Helmut Humbach · Pallan Ichaporia

The Heritage of Zarathushtra

A NEW TRANSLATION OF HIS GĀTHĀS

HEIDELBERG 1994

UNIVERSITÄTSVERLAG C. WINTER

Die Deutsche Bibliothek - CIP-Einheitsaufnahme

Zarathustra:

The heritage of Zarathushtra: a new translation of his Gathas / [Zarathushtra]. Helmut Humbach; Pallan Ichaporia. - Heidelberg: Winter, 1994

Einheitssacht.: Gāthā
ISBN 3-8253-0251-2

NE: Humbach, Helmut [Hrsg.]; HST

ISBN 3-8253-0251-2

Imprimé en Allemagne. Printed in Germany
Druck: Strauss Offsetdruck GmbH, 69509 Mörlenbach

Table of Contents

Technical Remarks

The Avestan text is transliterated according to the now standard system introduced by Karl Hoffmann. The spelling of proper names and religious terms has been simplified, however, in the Introduction as well as in the English translation. The text is that of K. F. Geldner's edition: *Avesta, The Sacred Books of the Parsis* I-III, Tübingen 1886. Departures from this norm are indicated by a postponed small circle (°) in the case of orthographic variants and given explicitely in the foot-notes when involving morphological differences.

Abbreviations etc.

OAv. = Old Avestan
(i.e. the language of the Yathā Ahū Vairiyō, the Ashem Vohū, the Gāthās, the Yasna Haptanghāiti, and the Ā Airyēmā Ishiyō)
YAv. = Young Avestan (i.e. the language of the Younger Avesta)

lit. = literally
ms. = manuscript
mss. = manuscripts
var. = variant reading found in one or more manuscripts
varr. = variant readings found in the manuscripts

In the Avestan text:
[ ] square brackets denote later additions to the text
< > pointed brackets denote loss of text or elements of text

In the English translation:
( ) round brackets are used to denote additions inserted for better intelligibility.

Preface

When Gāthā scholarship began in the second half of the 19th century knowledge of the grammar of the language was still rudimentary and the translations by necessity less than adequate. At best they reflected the Sasanians' understanding of the text as seen in the Pahlavi rendering, of uncertain date. Nevertheless, theories that were based on these early, mostly incorrect, translations remained the basis for subsequent translations of the Gāthās, thus producing a vicious circle which was broken only in the late 1950's. But even after this time Gāthā translations have tended to cater to a public expecting traditional renderings and an easily readable text, although such translations can only be achieved by smoothing over numerous difficulties in the text or plainly disregarding the grammar.

The first to study the Gāthās applying the rigorous methods of modern philology was Helmut Humbach, *Die Gathas des Zarathustra* I-II, Heidelberg 1959, an updated English version of which is his *The Gāthās of Zarathushtra* I-II, Heidelberg 1991.

While these two earlier translations to a great extent mirror the Avestan text in all its complexities, the present version is intended to be user-friendly and to be consulted by those who prefer an easier access to the Gāthās as poetry and religious document. We have tried to accomplish this without departing too much from the original text, but also without encumbering the translation with stylistic features common in Avestan but alien to English.

In this way we hope we have avoided creating misunderstandings at the same time as making the text readily available to those who wish to study it for its vocabulary and phraseology or for its message.

For scholars this new translation does not replace the two earlier editions, which should be consulted for philological details as well as for Helmut Humbach's personal opinions regarding Zarathushtra and his Religion.

Helmut Humbach wishes to thank his old friend and colleague, Prods Oktor Skjærvø (Harvard University) for taking time to read this translation, as well, and to discuss with him numerous details of it.

August, 1st, 1994

Helmut Humbach
Universität, FB 14
D 55099 Mainz, Germany

Pallan Ichaporia
253 South 4th Street
Womelsdorf Pa 19567, USA

Introduction

1. Zarathushtra

1. According to Xanthos, a Greek historian of Lydian descent who wrote in the mid-5th century B.C., Spitama Zarathushtra (Zaraϑuštra), the prophet of Ancient Iran, lived 600 years before Xerxes' crossing of the Hellespont (480 + 600 = 1080 B.C.). This is in approximate agreement with the linguistic evidence. The native Iranian tradition, transmitted by sources of the early Islamic period (i.e., more than one millennium later) puts him 300 years before Alexander's campaign (330 + 300 = 630 B.C.).[1]

1.1. By Xanthos or, rather, one of his unknown sources, the name of the prophet was distorted into Zōroastrēs (whence Latin Zoroaster), thus wrongly linking him with the Chaldaean astrologers.

1.2. Zarathushtra mentions his own name fifteen times in his Gāthās (Gāϑās), once in the first person (46,19 'for me, Zarathushtra'), once he adresses himself rhetorically (46,14 'O Zarathushtra'). He quotes the following persons among his adherents and relations, or addresses them: Kavi Vishtāspa, his princely promoter, Frashaoshtra Hvōguva and Jāmāspa Hvōguva, two noble brothers at Vishtāspa's court, Maidyōimāngha Spitama, Zarathushtra's cousin who was later said to have been his first convert, the clan of the Haēchataspa Spitamas, relatives of the prophet, Zarathushtri Spitāma, a son of the prophet whose individual name is left unmentioned, and the prophet's youngest daughter Pouruchistā Haēchataspānā Spitāmī. Honorable mention is also made of the relations and descendants of Tūra son of Friya, perhaps a member of a Turanian family.

1.3. By granting Zarathushtra shelter at his court, which was an essential prerequisite for the spreading of the Religion, Kavi Vishtāspa 'Prince Vishtāspa' stood out among the many rulers who opposed the prophet, called by him 'the (other) Kavis'. In the same context as these, the Karapans, the Usijs, and the Grehma gang are mentioned, groups of religious or political character that are otherwise not defined. Two opponents of the prophet are blamed by him individually for not having accepted him, namely Vaēpiya the Kaviyan (51,12) and Bendva (49,1) whom he ironically calls a 'great chief'.

1.4. The society described by Zarathushtra was organized in house, village, county (or: district), and land (or: country). The members of a household are a family, the inhabitants of a village are a community (or: clan), those of a county are a tribe (or: people of the county). No term for the inhabitants of a land is found. In this society the power and renown of individuals as well as of social groups could be measured in the number of sheep, oxen, horses, and camels, owned by them, as well as in the pasture area they commanded and its fertility. The food of average people was mostly barley,

[1] By a lapsus in *The Gāthās* I, 1991, p. 26, the Greek number of years as written in the Istanbul manuscript is given as hexēkonta '600' instead of hexakosia '600'.

milk, and milk products, occasionally meat. Yet many people experienced difficulties living from day to day in infertile mountains and steppes and grazing their cattle in poor soil under hard climatic conditions.

1.5. In the time of Zarathushtra the tribes were constantly engaged in warfare. The Kavis other than Kavi Vishtāspa flourished and prospered by raiding and plundering the pastoral and agricultural settlements. Their priests worshipped a pantheon of divinities called Daēvas, the ancient gods, interpreted by Zarathushtra as false gods, devils or demons. Through cruel bloody sacrifices and ritual partaking of intoxicants, preferably strong forms of the Haoma (Haoma Dūraosha), they would seek the help of the Daēvas for the success of the raids perpetrated by their worldly leaders. Against their religious views, called by him a religion of deceit (Druj), Zarathushtra set the Mazdayasnian Religion, the worship of Ahura Mazdā, who represents the principle of truth (Asha/Aša), the foremost in a long series of other Ahurian principles or moral concepts (see 2.2). He rejected and condemned the Daēvas and all their adherents, who ruined existence, and he wished the aggressive chieftains of the deceitful tribes of the neighborhood to be replaced by peaceful good rulers such as truthful Kavi Vishtāspa.

2. The Mazdayasnian Religion

2.1. Zarathushtra's Religion is considered by scholars as the dualistic religion par excellence, i.e., a religion in which the evil in the world is not attributed to God's inscrutable ways, as is necessary in monotheism, but in which God's antagonists are blamed for it. As a matter of fact, the life of the world from the loss of paradise caused by Yima[1] to its renovation is painted in the Zarathushtrian tradition as a continuous conflict between Ahura Mazdā and the Daēvas and their respective ideals, between the principle of truth (Asha/Aṣ̌a) and that of deceit (Druj), between good and evil, between the truthful and the deceitful. Yet, for the following reason the dualistic interpretation must be somewhat modified: In the Gāthās Ahura Mazdā is described as being at the head of a group of divine beings called Ahuras. These Ahuras evidently are the antagonists of the Daēvas, but among the latter there is no individual antagonist of Ahura Mazdā, such as the Evil Spirit in the Younger Avesta (Angra Mainyu) and the Middle and New Persian literature (Ahreman). This is a very monotheistic aspect of Zarathushtra's spiritual world. The picture of the end of this material world drawn by the prophet is even purely monotheistic. By the renovation and transfiguration of the world called its 'brilliant-making', Ahura Mazdā and the truthful guided by the prophet will finally succeed in eliminating evil, restoring paradise on earth, and securing Ahura Mazdā's rule for ever.

2.2. The Ahuras, a group of spiritual entities, are described best as personifications of the Ahurian principles and concepts. These principles and concepts are designated by what we call Ahurian terms. Apart from truth (Asha for which see 1.5), they include holy spirit (Spenta Mainyu), good spirit (Vohu Mainyu), good thought (Vohu Manah), good power (Vohu Khshathra), power worthy of being chosen (Khshathra Vairiya), right-mindedness (Ārmaiti), obedience/attention (Sraosha), integrity (Haurvatāt) and

[1] Yima, YAv. also Yima Xšaēta, New Persian Jamshīd.

immortality (Ameretatāt, Ameretāt), but also fire (Ātar) and good reward (Vanghvī Ashi). The Ahurian principles and concepts represent cosmic powers pervading both the spiritual and the material world and manifesting themselves in both the divine and human sphere. Thus Asha does not only denote the Ahurian principle and concept 'truth' but also its realization as a moral quality of Ahura Mazdā as well as of his truthful worshippers. It also not only denotes its personification as a divine entity but also its materialization in the good things of the world, then called 'material truth' (Astvat Ashem).

2.2.1. To the Ahurian principles and concepts, the dualistic picture of the world opposes the corresponding Daēvic concepts such as deceit (Druj), harmful spirit (Angra Mainyu), evil spirit (Aka Mainyu), evil thought (Aka Manah), scorn (Tarōmaiti), disobedience (Asrushti), and others, such as wrath (Aēšma).

2.2.2. The number of both the Ahurian terms and their Daēvic counterparts is undefined in the Gāthās. That of the Ahurian terms has been noticeably enlarged in the Yasna Haptanghāiti (3.2.2). Six of them are represented as Holy Immortals (Amesha Spentas) in the Younger Avesta, where they are the patron saints of the six working days of the first week of each month: namely, good thought (Vohu Manah), best truth (Asha Vahishta), power worthy of being chosen (Khshathra Vairiya), holy right-mindedness (Spentā Ārmaiti), integrity (Haurvatāt), and immortality (Ameretatāt). The term 'Holy Immortals' (Amesha Spenta) is not attested in the Gāthās, but the Yasna Haptanghāiti twice speaks of Spenta Ameshas with an inversion of the two elements, with which we can perhaps compare the inverted word order Mazdā Ahura found beside Ahura Mazdā in both the Gāthās and the Yasna Haptanghāiti.

3. The Gathas and the other Old Avestan texts

3.1. Zarathushtra's Gāthās (Gāϑās) are preserved in the Yasna, the liturgy of the Zarathushtrians. Small groups of these survive in Iran, but their best-known branch is the Pārsis ("Persians") in India, particularly in Bombay, and in Pakistan. These are descendants of Iranian emigrants of the medieval period. In the past decades numerous groups of Zarathushtrians, Iranian as well as Indian and Pakistani, have established themselves in America and Europe.

3.2. The Gāthā collection forms the core of the Yasna liturgy which is about two fifths of what has come down to us of the Avesta, the Holy Scriptures of the Zarathushtrians. The Gāthās consist of seventeen religious hymns each of them covering one chapter (Hāiti) of the Yasna (Yasna 28-34, 43-51, 53).

3.2.1. Avestan, the language of the Avesta, is an Old Iranian language closely related to Old Persian known from the Achaemenid inscriptions. Avestan is attested in two dialects differing from each other both chronologically and dialectologically. Whereas most of the Avesta is in Young Avestan dialect the Gāthas are composed in the archaic dialect we call Old Avestan.

3.2.2. Old Avestan is also used in the Yasna Haptanghāiti (Haptaŋhāiti), the 'Yasna of Seven Chapters', a prose text inserted in the Gāthās (Yasna 35-41) and attributed by most scholars to early successors of the prophet.

3.2.3. Old Avestan features are also found in what the Zarathushtrians call their four Most Holy Prayers, namely the triad which precedes the Gāthās: the Yathā Ahū Vairiyō (Yaϑā Ahū Vairiiō,Yasna 27,13), the Ashem Vohū (Ašəm Vohū, Yasna 27,14), and the Yenghē Hātām (Yeŋ́hē Hātąm, Yasna 27,15), and the Ā Airyemā Ishiyō (Ā Airiiəmā Išiiō, Yasna 54,1), which concludes them. Among these the Ā Airyemā Ishiyō is the only prayer in the strict sense of the word; the other three are better characterized as manthras (Middle Persian nīrang, cf. Sanskrit mantra), that is, powerful meditational texts and truth-spells.

3.2.4. Among these four prayers or manthras, the Yathā Ahū Vairiyō, the Ashem Vohū, and the Ā Airyemā Ishiyō are in pure Old Avestan dialect. Thus there is no reason for questioning Zarathushtra's authorship of them. As a matter of fact it is hardly thinkable that the founder of a religion left his adherents without any manthras or prayers. Only the authorship of the Yenghē Hātām is somewhat doubtful. The only Old Avestan characteristic found here is the lengthening of the final vowels of the single words whereas the words themselves appear in a typically Young Avestan form. Thus yenghē (yeŋ́hē), the first word of the Yenghē Hātām (Yeŋ́hē Hātąm), is most instructive. It equals Young Avestan yeŋ́he, but contrasts with its correct Old Avestan equivalent yehiiā. From this it is evident that our Yenghē Hātām, inspite of the Old Avestan appearance of its word endings, must have had a Young Avestan original. On the other hand, the name of God is given there not in its Young Avestan form Ahura Mazdā but with the Gāthic word order Mazdā Ahura. Thus one is entitled to concludé that the dialectal inconsistencies of the language of the Yenghē Hātām do not necessarily prove a post-Gāthic origin of the stanza. Instead they may be due to a complicated textual history.

3.3. The term Gāthā is often used to designate each of the seventeen hymns which form the seventeen Hāitis or chapters of the Gāthā collection, and this use has even found its way into numerous scholarly publications. However, in scholarly usage the term Gāthā should be used exclusively to denote one of the five groups in which the seventeen hymns are arranged according to their respective meters:

(1) Ahunavaitī Gāthā (Ahunauuaitī Gāϑā), seven hymns (Yasna 28-34). Stanzas of three lines of regularly 7+9 or 7+8 syllables each.

(2) Ushtavaitī Gāthā (Uštauuaitī Gāϑā), four hymns (Yasna 43-46). Stanzas of five lines of regularly 4+7 sylllables each.

(3) Spentāmainyu Gāthā (Spəṇtāmainiiu Gāϑā), four hymns (Yasna 47-50). Stanzas of four lines of regularly 4+7 syllables each.

(4) Vohukhshathrā Gāthā (Vohuxšaϑrā Gāϑā), one hymn only (Yasna 51). Stanzas of three lines of regularly 7+7 syllables each.

(5) Vahishtōishti Gāthā (Vahištōišti Gāϑā), one hymn only (Yasna 53). Stanzas of four lines (but 53,6 five lines) of undefined number each.

4. The authenticity of the transmitted text

4.1. The text of the Avesta is transmitted in an alphabetical script including vowels which was created in Sasanian times with the purpose of exactly rendering and preserving the phonetic peculiarities of the pronunciation of the oral tradition as codified by the Sasanian redaction of the Avesta. Yet, linguistic considerations suggest that, particularly with regard to the vowels, the Sasanian way of recitation did no longer agree in all details with Zarathushtra's pronunciation. Numerous dissyllabic vowels or diphthongs had been reduced to monosyllabic value, and numerous redundant vowels had been developed. Thus dayanā/daiianā 'religious view, religion' had been reduced to daēnā, and shyaothna/š́iiaoϑna 'action, act, deed' had been extended to shyaothana/š́iiaoϑana (a development which has continued to modern times where, e.g., the ritual pronunciation of the noun khshathra/xšaϑra 'power', though preserved correctly in its written form, has developed into khashathra). Such phonetic change took place unconsciously, adapting itself to the phonetic pecularities of the respective contemporary language. It did not, however, affect the substance of the text, although it must be taken into account for a correct evaluation of the number of syllables in a Gāthic line.

4.2. According to a syntactic rule largely observed in the archaic language of the Gāthās, verbal prefixes can stand separated from their verb, e.g., in Y 50,9 paitī ... aiienī 'I shall approach again' (instead of connected paitī.aiienī or paitiiaiienī). In a number of cases the separated prefix has been repeated immediately before the verb so that the text has the separated as well as the connected preverb, e.g., in Y 48,7 paitī ... paitī.siiōdūm 'strike (your axe)'. In such cases the repeated prefix is metrically redundant, a fact which proves that the repetition does not belong to the original text but must have been inserted by the Sasanian, or perhaps by an earlier redaction, in order to make the text easier to understand. To restore Zarathushtra's original the repeated preverb evidently must be suppressed. In this edition it is placed in square brackets, writing paitī ... [paitī.]siiōdūm. This insertion, as well, did not affect the substance of the text.

4.3. The metrical regularity of by far most of the Gāthic lines has led the majority of Gāthic scholars to "correct" the transmitted text of all, many, or parts of Gāthic lines that are metrically irregular, having one syllable too much or too less. The most common example of this procedure is Y 28,6c yā daibišuuatō duuaēšå tauruuaiiāma 'whereby we may overcome the hostilities of the enemy'. The number of syllables of the line exceeds the norm, having 10 instead of regularly 8/9 syllables. There is therefore among scholars a strong presumption that the text is corrupt. To "correct" it some delete duuaēšå, obtaining 8 syllables, others obtain 9 syllables by replacing tauruuaiiāmā with tauruuāmā otherwise not attested in Avestan. Neither of the two solutions is acceptable. It is much more likely that the text is correctly transmitted and that Zarathushtra used, without regard for the number of syllables, a set phrase which exceeded the bounds of the meter.

5. Notes on the poetry of the Gāthās

5.1. From the translations presented here it will be seen — and it may come as a surprise to some — that some of the concepts attributed to Zarathushtra by modern scholarship such as the "myth of the two spirits" actually are not found in the Gāthās. The two passages in question (30,3-4, 45,2) in fact describe the choices that have to be made by any person at any time. Of special interest is the exact interpretation in which integrity (Haurvatāt/Hauruuatāt) and immortality (Ameretatāt/Amərətatāt) are depicted as sacrificial offerings (33,8.12, 34,1.11, 44,19, 45,10, 47,1). On the one hand this usage goes back to the Indo-European and Indo-Iranian times (cf. Greek Ambrosia and Sanskrit Amrita, both of which have the double meaning 'immortality' and 'elixir of life as enjoyed by the gods for food'). On the other hand it continues in the Younger Avesta where the two words denote the liquid and vegetable parts of the oblation. As for the Gāthic use we just must leave open the question which kind of offerings are referred to by Zarathushtra.

5.2. It should also be stressed that the Gāthās are not a religious handbook with carefully co-ordinated paragraphs. Thus in 30,6 the Daēvas are said to be used to choosing the worst thought and wrath of the deceitful, whereas in 32,1 they are depicted as being out to take possession of the pious gifts offered to Ahura Mazdā by the truthful. There is also an apparent contradiction between the translation of 31,1 given here where Zarathushtra proclaims unheard words to the deceitful, and 31,18 where he expresses the wish that no adherent of the deceitful one should be allowed to listen to Ahura Mazdā's manthras and teachings. Yet in this case at least we can see that the apparent contradiction is not necessarily an actual one. The prophet doubtlessly distinguishes between adherents of the alien faith who can and cannot be taught the new faith. The problem lies with the poetic style, which allows him to vaguely allude to or even completely omit the details we would regard as the most relevant.

5.3. Although the Gāthās are poetical texts of visionary character they are composed according to rules of a poetical technique which were in vogue at the prophet's time. Modern readers are unaccustomed to this technique, and they must train themselves to understand it. In a number of passages, Zarathushtra's intoning a song of praise is compared with somebody yoking a team of horses (28,10, 30,10, 50,6-7). Other similes derive from the world of ideas of the cattle-breeders. Thus the 'bulls of the days' mentioned in 46,3 stand metaphorically for the first rays of the rosy dawn, announcing the rosy dawn itself which is implicitly compared with a herd of cows. On the other hand the bulls of the days announcing the morning are parallel with the 'intellects of the strengtheners' or 'intellects of the Saoshyants', i.e., with the wise decisions of the promoters and sponsors of the Religion, who are expected to play a decisive part in the 'brilliant-making', that is, the renovation and transfiguration of the world.

The Gāthās of Zarathushtra

The Holy Prayers of the Zarathushtrians

and

The Yasna Haptanghāiti

Text and Translation

Yasna 27,13-15. Introductory Prayers

27,13. Yaϑā Ahū Vairiiō

Yaϑā ahū vairiiō   aϑā ratuš aṣ̌āt̰cīt̰ hacā
vaŋhəuš dazdā manaŋhō   š́iiaoϑənanąm[1] aŋhəuš mazdāi
xšaϑrəmcā ahurāi.ā   yim drigubiiō dadat̰ vāstārəm

[1] Geldner š́iiaoϑananąm as usual in the manuscript transmission of the Gāthās.

Yasna 27,13-15. Introductory Prayers

27,13. Yathā Ahū Vairiyō

Since He is (the One) to be chosen by the world
therefore the judgment emanating from truth itself
(to be passed) on the deeds of good thought of the world,
as well as the power, is committed to Mazdā Ahura whom (people) assign
as a shepherd to the poor.[1]

[1] More literally: 'Since/as He is to be chosen by the world therefore/so the judgment emanating from truth itself (to be passed) on the deeds of good thought of the world is committed to Mazdā (Ahura), and the power (is committed) to (Mazdā) Ahura...'. Note the repetitions 'world ... world' and 'commit ... assign' (lit. 'give ... give'). With its artistic syntax the Yathā Ahū Vairiyō offers a summary of the Zarathushtrian Religion in three lines. The traditional translation of its first line by 'as He is the Lord so He is the judge' is attested as early as in the Younger Avesta (cf. particularly Y 19.12). Yet it is untenable for both grammatical and syntactical reasons. A more reliable picture results from comparison with Yasht 19,12.90. There the phrase aϑa ratuš 'such/so (is) the judgment' refers to eschatological events which suggests that the Yathā Ahū Vairiyō has an eschatological reference as well.

27,14. Aṣ̌əm Vohū

Aṣ̌əm vohū vahištəm astī
uštā astī uštā ahmāi
hiiat̰ aṣ̌āi vahištāi aṣ̌əm

27,15. Yeŋ́hē Hātąm

Yeŋ́hē hātąm āat̰ yesnē paitī vaŋhō[1]
mazdā̊ ahurō vaēϑā[2] aṣ̌āt̰ hacā yā̊ŋhąmcā
tąscā tā̊scā yazamaidē

[1] The Vulgata reading vaŋhō (instead of expected vaŋ́hō) is also found in Vispered 16,3 yaēṣ̌ąm nō ahurō mazdā̊ aṣ̌auua yesne paiti vaŋhō vaēδa. The Vispered passage is modelled after the Yenghē Hātam, but the Young Avestan dialect form vaēϑa is replaced there by the standard form vaēδa as well as the archaic word order mazdā̊ ahurō is replaced by the Young Avestan standard ahurō mazdā̊.

27,14. Ashem Vohū

Truth is best (of all that is) good.
As desired, what is being desired
is truth for Him/him who (represents) best truth.

or:

Truth is best (of all that is) good.
As desired, as desired, truth
is for Him/him who (represents) best truth.[1]

Yasna 27,15. Yenghē Hātām

In accordance with truth Mazdā Ahura knows the man among the existing,
as well as the women, whose better (attitude is seen) at worship.[2]
Those men and women[3] we worship.

---

[1] The Ashem Vohū consists of three lines of four words each. Note the repetitions 'truth ... truth ... truth', 'good ... best ... best', 'desired ... desired'. The first of the two Ushtā's doubtlessly means 'as desired', but the second is ambiguous as it can mean 'as desired' as well as 'what is being desired' (cf. 43,1). Thus at least two different renderings of the Ashem Vohū are possible. Zarathushtra may even have intended the ambiguities to provide a basis for the pious to meditate on the message of the stanza.

[2] lit.: 'In accordance with truth Mazdā Ahura knows the better (attitude) of which male one among the existing, and of which female ones, (has been seen) at worship.'

[3] 'those men and women', lit. 'those male ones and those female ones'. The text recalls 51,22, but it is not clear whether its third line refers to the Ahuras (Amesha Spentas), or to human beings, or to both.

Yasna 28-34. Ahunauuaiti Gāϑā

[Yānīm manō yānīm vacō yānīm š́iiaoϑnəm aṣ̌aonō zaraϑuštrahe][1]
[Fərā aməṣ̌ā spəṇtā gāϑā̊ gə̄uruuāin]

[Nəmō və̄ gāϑā̊ aṣ̌aonīš][2]

Yasna 28. Ahiiāsā Hāiti

28,1. Ahiiā yāsā nəmaŋhā ustānazastō rafəδrahiiā
mainiiə̄uš° mazdā pouruuīm spəṇtahiiā aṣ̌ā vīspəṇg š́iiaoϑanā
vaŋhə̄uš xratūm manaŋhō yā xšnəuuīšā gə̄uščā uruuānəm

28,2. yə̄ vā̊ mazdā ahurā pairī.jasāi vohū manaŋhā
maibiiōi dāuuōi ahuuā̊ astuuatascā hiiat̰cā manaŋhō
āiiaptā aṣ̌āt̰ hacā yāiš rapəṇtō° daidīt̰ xᵛāϑrē

28,3. yə̄ vā̊ aṣ̌ā ufiiānī manascā vohū apaouruuīm
mazdąmcā ahurəm yaēibiiō xšaϑrəmcā aγžō.nuuamnəm°
varədaitī ārmaitiš ā mōi rafəδrāi zauuəṇg jasatā

28,4. yə̄ uruuānəm mə̄ṇ‹g›[3] gairē vohū dadē haϑrā manaŋhā
aṣ̌īšcā š́iiaoϑananąm vīduš mazdā̊ ahurahiiā
yauuat̰ isāi tauuācā auuat̰ xsāi aēšē aṣ̌ahiiā

28,5. aṣ̌ā kat̰ ϑβā darəsānī manascā vohū vaēdəmnō
gātūmcā ahurāi səuuištāi° səraošəm mazdāi
anā mąϑrā mazištəm vāurōimaidī xrafstrā hizuuā

28,6. vohū gaidī manaŋhā dāidī aṣ̌ā dā̊ darəgāiiū
ərəšuuāiš tū uxδāiš mazdā zaraϑuštrāi aojōŋhuuat̰° rafənō
ahmaibiiācā ahurā yā daibišuuatō duuaēšā̊ tauruuaiiāmā

28,7. dāidī aṣ̌ā tąm aṣ̌īm vaŋhə̄uš āiiaptā manaŋhō
dāidī tū ārmaitē vīštāspāi īšəm maibiiācā
dā̊stū mazdā xšaiiācā yā və̄ mąϑrā srəuuīmā° rādā̊[4]

---

[1] The first of these three lines has been inserted in the Young Avestan period.
[2] The second and third lines are in Old Avestan dialect but they are of post-Zarathushtrian origin.
[3] məṇ gairē instead of məṇg gairē, owing to erroneous segmentation of spoken text.
[4] srəuuīmā rādā̊, Geldner srəuuīm ārādā̊.

Yasna 28-34. Ahunavaitī Gāthā

[Of truthful Zarathushtra the thoughts, words, and actions are entreating.]
[May the Holy Immortals accept the Gāthās.]

[Reverence to you, O truthful Gāthās.]

Yasna 28. Ahiyāsā Hāiti

28,1. In reverence for him, with hands out-stretched at first I entreat (you) all, O Mazdā, for the actions of support of the spirit holy through truth, through whom you may gratify the intellect of good thought[1] and the soul of the cow.

28,2. I approach you with good thought, O Mazdā Ahura, so that you may grant me (the blessings) of the two existences, the material and that of thought, the blessings emanating from truth, with which one can put (your) supporters in comfort

28,3. I extol you as never before, O truth, and good thought and Mazdā Ahura, for (all of) whom right-mindedness increases also unfading power. May you come to my calls for support.

28,4. Inspired by good thought and being a witness for Mazdā Ahura, I have in mind (one's) soul for (his commendation by my) song, as well as the rewards for (his) actions. For as long as I can and am able I shall look out in (my) search for truth.

28,5. O truth, shall I see you, I who possess good thought as well as obedience to be a throne for Him, the very strong Mazdā Ahura? O you beasts,[2] through this manthra, (spoken) by (my) tongue, we would win (Him), the Greatest one.

28,6. Come with good thought. With truth grant (us) a long-lasting gift through your exalted utterances, O Mazdā Ahura. (Grant it) as strong support to Zarathushtra and to us all so that thereby we may overcome the hostilities of (your) enemy.

28,7. Grant us that reward, O truth, the blessings of good thought. Grant, O right-mindedness, vigor to Vishtāspa and me. Grant (these things), O Mazdā, and rule with a manthra through which we can learn of your bounties.

---

[1] 'intellect of good thought' instead of 'men (and women) possessing the intellect of good thought'.

[2] The beasts (or: noxious animals) include the Daēvas and the (evil) mortals, cf. 34,5. They are addressed here in order to discourage and chase them away from the ritual so as not to spoil it.

28,8. vahištəm ϑβā vahištā yə̄m aṣ̌ā vahištā hazaošəm
ahurəm yāsā vāunuš narōi fərašaoštrāi maibiiācā
yaēibiiascā īṯ rå̄ŋhaŋhōi vīspāi yauuē vaŋhə̄uš manaŋhō

28,9. anāiš vå̄ nōiṯ ahurā mazdā aṣ̌əmcā yānāiš zaranaēmā
manascā hiiaṯ vahištəm yōi və̄ yōiϑəmā dasəmē stūtąm
yūžə̄m zəuuīštiiå̄ŋhō īšō xšaϑrəmcā sauuaŋhąm

28,10. aṯ yə̄ṇg aṣ̌āaṯcā vōistā vaŋhə̄ušcā dāϑə̄ṇg manaŋhō
ərəϑβə̄ṇg mazdā ahurā aēibiiō pərənā āpanāiš kāməm
aṯ və̄ xšmaibiiā asūnā vaēdā xᵛaraiϑiiā vaiṇtiiā srauuå̄

28,11. yə̄ āiš aṣ̌əm nipå̄ŋ́hē° manascā vohū yauuaētāitē
tuuə̄m mazdā ahurā frō mā sīšā ϑβahmāṯ vaocaŋ́hē°
mainiiə̄uš° hacā ϑβā ə̄əå̄ŋhā yāiš ā aŋhuš pouruiiō bauuaṯ[1]

End of Yasna 28

[1] bauuaṯ perhaps slightly incorrect for buuaṯ.

28,8. I lovingly ask you, O Best one, the Ahura who is in harmony with best truth, for that which is best for gentle Frashaoshtra, and for me, and for all those on whom you will bestow it with good thought for all time.

28,9. With these entreaties, O Mazdā Ahura, may we not anger you, nor truth or best thought, we who are standing at the offering of praises to you. You are the swiftest (bringers of) invigorations, and (you hold) the power over the benefits.

28,10. Fulfill with gains the desire of those whom you know to be just and meticulous through truth and good thought, O Mazdā Ahura. For (all of) you, O Rich ones, I know loving eulogies conducted by a good charioteer.[1]

28,11. Through these you store for yourself truth and good thought for eternity, O Mazdā Ahura. So teach me with your mouth, in accordance with your spirit, how to pronounce these (eulogies) by which the first existence comes into being.[2]

End of Yasna 28

[1] 'conducted by a good charioteer': The eulogies are compared with a team competing at a horse-race (cf. 30,10, 50,6-7; Introd. 5,3). Thus 'good charioteer' is the well-trained tongue of the singer.

[2] 'the first existence comes into being', or: 'came into being', or: 'will come into being'? Instead of 'first existence' perhaps better 'foremost existence'. At any rate, in the Gāthās 'first' when used in connection with 'existence' has a wide spectrum of meanings.

Yasna 29. Xšmāuuōiia.gə̄uš.uruuā Hāiti

29,1. Xšmaibiiā gə̄uš uruuā gərəždā kahmāi mā ϑβarōždūm kə̄ mā tašat̰
ā mā aēšəmō hazascā rəmō [ā]hišāiiā dərəšcā təuuišcā
nōit̰ mōi vāstā xšmat̰ aniiō aϑā mōi sąstā vohū vāstriiā

29,2. adā tašā gə̄uš pərəsat̰ aṣ̌əm kaϑā tōi gauuōi ratuš
hiiat̰ hīm dātā xšaiiaṇtō hadā vāstrā gaodāiiō ϑβaxšō
kə̄m hōi uštā ahurəm yə̄ drəguuō.dəbīš° aēšəməm vādāiiōit̰

29,3. ahmāi aṣ̌ā nōit̰ sarəjā aduuaēšō gauuōi paitī.mrauuat̰
auuaēšąm nōit̰ vīduiiē yā šauuaitē[1] ādrə̄ṇg ərəšuuā̊ŋhō
hātąm huuō aojištō yahmāi zauuə̄ṇg jimā kərədušā

29,4. mazdā̊ saxᵛārə̄ mairištō yā zī vāuuərəzōi pairī ciϑīt̰
daēuuāišcā maṣ̌iiāišcā yācā varəšaitē aipī ciϑīt̰
huuō vīcirō ahurō aϑā nə̄ aŋhat̰ yaϑā huuō vasat̰

29,5. at̰ vā ustānāiš ahuuā zastāiš frīnəmnā ahurāi.ā
mə̄ uruuā gə̄ušcā aziiā̊ hiiat̰ mazdąm duuaidī fərasā̊biiō[2]
nōit̰ ərəžəjiiōi frajiiāitiš nōit̰ fsuiieṇtē drəguuasū pairī

29,6. at̰ ‹h›ə̄ vaocat̰ ahurō mazdā̊ vīduuā̊ vafūš viiānaiiā
nōit̰ aēuuā ahū vistō naēdā ratuš aṣ̌āt̰cīt̰ hacā
at̰ zī ϑβā fšuiiaṇtaēcā vāstriiāicā ϑβōrəštā tatašā

29,7. tə̄m āzūtōiš ahurō mąϑrəm tašat̰ aṣ̌ā hazaošō
mazdā̊ gauuōi xšuuīdəmcā huuō urušaēibiiō spəṇtō sāsnaiiā
kastē vohū manaŋhā yə̄ ī dāiiāt̰ ə̄əāuuā marətaēibiiō

29,8. aēm mōi idā vistō yə̄ nə̄ aēuuō sāsnā̊ gūšatā
zaraϑuštrō spitāmō huuō nə̄ mazdā vaštī aṣ̌āicā
carəkərəϑrā srāuuaiieŋ́hē hiiat̰ hōi hudəmə̄m diiāi vaxəδrahiia

29,9. at̰cā gə̄uš uruuā raostā yə̄ anaēšəm xšąnmə̄nē rādəm
vācəm nərəš asūrahiiā yə̄m ā vasəmī īšā.xšaϑrīm
kadā yauuā huuō aŋhat̰ yə̄ hōi dadat̰ zastauuat̰ auuō

---

[1] šauuaitē, mss. šauuaitē and ṣ̌auuaitē.
[2] fərasā̊biiō, Geldner fərasābiiō.

Yasna 29. Khshmāvōiia-gēush-urvā Hāiti

29,1. The soul of the cow[1] complains to you: "For whom did you shape me? Who fashioned me? Wrath and oppression, fury, spite, and violence hold me fettered. I have no shepherd other than you. Thus reveal yourselves to me with good pastoral work."

29,2. Thereupon the fashioner of the cow asks truth: "Of what kind is your judgment for the cow? As you, O Ruling ones, have ordered zealous cattle-breeding together with forage, whom do you wish to be her master who may crush the wrath of the deceitful?"

29,3. But no deliverer will answer (the fashioner) through truth in a way helpful to the cow. No one knows how to set the weak free. He is the strongest among the existing, (the Ahura), whom I wish to reach with (the plaintiff) who has called (for help).[2]

29,4. May Mazdā who precisely remembers acts of brutality take note here and now those which have been perpetrated by Daēvas and (evil) mortals, and may he hereafter take note of those which will be perpetrated by them in future. He is the Ahura with judicial authority. As He desires, so it shall be for us.

29,5. Therefore we two, my soul and that of the fertile cow,[3] are devoting ourselves mindfully and with hands out-stretched to Mazdā Ahura, choosing Him to give (us) orders. There is no hope for the cattle-breeder living correctly among the deceitful.

29,6. Mazdā Ahura, knowing the pronouncements through His vitality, says (to the cow): "No judgment emanating from truth itself has been found by the world. For the shaper has fashioned you for the cattle-breeding herdsman."

29,7. In harmony with truth, Mazdā Ahura, by His teaching beneficial to the emaciated, fashioned for the cow both the manthra of nourishment and the milk. Who may be able through good thought to send these things down to the mortals?

29,8. Here, I have found Zarathushtra Spitama, the only one who listens to our teachings: He wishes to sing hymns of praise for us, O Mazdā, and for truth, to let me enjoy the beauty of his speech.

29,9. But the soul of the cow laments: "Must I be content with a vigorless caretaker, with the voice of a weak man while I wish him to be in possession of vigorous power? When will that person ever come who can offer him help with (his own) hand?"

---

[1] 'soul of the cow' is a mystical concept. It encompasses the soul of the primeval animal as well as that of the whole species and that of any living member of that species. In the present context it particularly refers to the soul of the animal that the deceitful have taken hold of in order to kill it cruelly for sacrificial purposes.

[2] 'whom I wish to reach ...' is uncertain. It seems that it is the soul of the cow which calls for help.

[3] 'my soul and that of the ... cow' is virtually the same as 'I, Zarathushtra, and the ... cow', cf. 50,1.

29,10. yūžəm aēibiio ahurā aogō dātā aṣ̌ā xšaϑrəmcā
auuat̰ vohū manaŋhā yā hušəitīš rāmąmcā dāt̰
azə̄mcīt̰ ahiiā mazdā ϑβąm mə̄ŋhī paouruuīm vaēdəm

29,11. kudā aṣ̌əm vohucā manō xšaϑrəmcā at̰ mā maṣ̌ā
yūžə̄m mazdā frāxšnənē mazōi magāi.ā paitī.zānatā
ahurā nū nā̊ auuarə̄ ə̄hmā rātōiš yūšmauuatąm

End of Yasna 29

29,10. Grant to those (present), O Mazdā Ahura, strength through truth and through good thought that power by which one may establish good dwellings and peace. Indeed I realize, that you are the first provider of these things.

29,11. Where are truth, good thought and power? Recognize me, (the cow), through (the mediation of) mortal (Zarathushtra), with foresight for the great offering. O Mazdā Ahura, come down to us now, on account of our gift to those such as you.

End of Yasna 29

Yasna 30. At̰.tā.vaxšiiā Hāiti

30,1. At̰ tā vaxšiiā išəṇtō yā mazdāϑā hiiat̰cīt̰ vīdušē
staotācā ahurāi yesniiāca vaŋhəuš manaŋhō
humązdrā āṣ̌ā.yecā[1] yā raocəbīš darəsatā uruuāzā

30,2. sraotā gəuš.āiš° vahištā auuaēnatā sūcā manaŋhā
āuuarənā̊ vīciϑahiiā narə̄m narəm xᵛaxiiāi tanuiiē
parā mazə̄ yā̊ŋhō ahmāi nə̄ sazdiiāi baodəṇtō° paitī

30,3. at̰ tā mainiiū pouruiiē yā yə̄mā xᵛafənā asruuātəm
manahicā vacahicā šiiaoϑanōi hī vahiiō akəmcā
ā̊scā hudā̊ŋhō ərəš vīšiiātā nōit̰ duždā̊ŋhō

30,4. at̰cā hiiat̰ tā hə̄m mainiiū jasaētəm paouruuīm dazdē
gaēmcā ajiiāitīmcā hiiatcā aŋhat̰ apə̄məm aŋhuš
acištō drəguuatąm at̰ aṣ̌āunē vahištəm manō

30,5. aiiā̊ mainiuuā̊° varatā yə̄ drəguuā̊ acištā vərəziiō
aṣ̌əm mainiiuš spə̄ništō yə̄ xraoždištə̄ṇg asə̄nō vastē
yaēcā xšnaošən ahurəm haiϑiiāiš šiiaoϑanāiš fraorət̰ mazdąm

30,6. aiiā̊ nōit̰ ərəš vīšiiātā daēuuācinā hiiat̰ īš ā dəbaomā
pərəs‹a›mnə̄ṇg[2] upā.jasat̰ hiiat̰ vərənātā acištəm manō
at̰ aēšəməm hə̄ṇduuārəṇtā yā bąnaiiən ahūm marətānō

30,7. ahmāicā xšaϑrā jasat̰ manaŋhā vohū aṣ̌ācā
at̰ kəhrpə̄m utaiiūitiš° dadāt̰ ārmaitiš ąnmā
aēšąm tōi ā aŋhat̰ yaϑā aiiaŋhā ādānāiš pouruiiō

30,8. at̰cā yadā aēšąm kaēnā jamaitī aēnaŋhąm
at̰ mazdā taibiiō xšaϑrəm vohū manaŋhā vōi.vīdāitī[3]
aēibiiō sastē ahurā yōi aṣ̌āi dadən zastaiiō drujəm

30,9. at̰cā tōi vaēm xiiāmā yōi īm fərašə̄m kərənaon[4] ahūm
mazdā̊scā ahurā̊ŋhō ā.mōiiastrā baranā aṣ̌ācā
hiiat̰ haϑrā manā̊ bauuat̰[5] yaϑrā cistiš aŋhat̰ maēϑā

---

[1] aṣ̌ā.yecā for aṣ̌aiia-cā from aṣ̌aiia-ca, or blunder for aṣ̌ā yaēca?
[2] pərəs‹a›mnə̄ṇg, Geldner pərəsmanə̄ṇg.
[3] vōi.vīdāitī, Geldner vōiuuīdāitī; varr. vōi.vīdāite, vōi.vīdaitī, vōi.vīdaite.
[4] kərənaon, Geldner kərənāun.
[5] bauuat̰, var. buuat̰.

Yasna 30. At-tā-vakhshyā Hāiti

30,1. O approaching ones, I shall now proclaim praises for the Ahura and worships of good thought, worthy of being noted even by Him who (already) knows them, O attentive ones, and for truth (I shall proclaim) the joy which is visible through the lights.

30,2. Hear the best with your ears. Through the radiance (of the fire) contemplate with your thought the preferences of decisions,[1] contemplate each man individually,[2] before the great sharing, in anticipation of having it proclaimed to us.

30,3. These are the two spirits (existing) in the beginning, twins who have been heard of as the two dreams, the two thoughts, the two words, and the two actions, the better and the evil. Between these two, the munificent discriminate rightly but not those who give bad gifts.

30,4. When these two spirits confront each other (to fight for a person,[3] then that person) determines (his) first (existence), (with) vitality or lack of vitality, and how his existence will be in the end. (The existence) of the deceitful will be very bad, but best thought will be (in store) for the truthful one.

30,5. Of these two spirits the deceitful one chooses to do the worst things, but the most holy spirit, clothed in the hardest stones, (chooses) truth, (as do those) who, with true actions, devotedly gratify Mazdā Ahura.

30,6. The Daēvas do not at all rightly discriminate between these two spirits, for as they take counsel with each other delusion comes over them, so that they choose the worst thought. In that way they all run to meet wrath, by which the mortals sicken existence.

30,7. And to this one He comes with power, good thought, and truth. Thus stability (grants) bodily form, and right-mindedness grants breath, and so by fettering the (Daēvas) in iron, (existence) will be your first one, O Ahura.

30,8. And so, when the (day of) payment for the crimes of these comes, (then) the power will be committed to you with good thought, O Mazdā Ahura, to command those who will deliver deceit into the hands of truth.

30,9. Thus may we be those who make existence brilliant, O Mazdā and you (other) Ahuras, with the bringing of changes, and with truth, while (our) thoughts are concentrated on the place where insight wavers.[4]

---

[1] 'preferences of decisions', or perhaps: 'invitations resulting from discernment' (cf. 45,1.8).

[2] Everybody who wants to participate in the worship of Ahura Mazdā has to undergo a test to determine whether he/she can be accepted.

[3] The two spirits fight with each other for each single person in order to win him or her over to their respective sides.

[4] 'where insight wavers': uncertain.

30,10. adā zī auuā drūjō [auuō.]bauuaitī[1] skəṇdō spaiiaϑrahiiā
at̰ asištā yaojaṇtē ā hušitōiš vaŋhə̄uš manaŋhō
mazdå aṣ̌ax́iiācā yōi zazəṇtī vaŋhāu srauuahī

30,11. hiiat̰ tā uruuātā saš́aϑā[2] yā mazdå dadāt̰ maṣ̌iiåŋhō
xᵛīticā ə̄nəitī hiiat̰cā darəgə̄m drəguuō.dəbiiō° rašō
sauuacā aṣ̌auuabiiō at̰ aipī tāiš aŋhaitī uštā

End of Yasna 30

---

[1] bauuaitī, var. buuaitī.
[2] saš́aϑā, Geldner saṣ̌aϑā without variants.

30,10. For then destruction will come down upon deceit through its elimination. The swiftest steeds will be yoked,[1] and they will win good fame (in the race) to the good dwelling of good thought, Mazdā, and truth.

30,11. O you mortals, when you observe the rules that Mazdā has established, for good behavior and about where not to go, and when (you consider) the long-lasting harm which is (in store) for the deceitful, and also the benefits for the truthful, then (you will realize that) by those (rules) the things desired will be there.

End of Yasna 30

[1] 'the swiftest steeds will be yoked': intonating a song of praise is compared with yoking a team of horses to a chariot for a horse-race (Introd. 5.3).

Yasna 31. Tā vō uruuātā Hāiti

31,1. Tā vō uruuātā marəṇtō aguštā vacā̊ sə̄ṇghāmahī
aēibiiō yōi uruuātāiš drūjō aṣ̌ahiiā gaēϑā̊ vīmərəṇcaitē
at̰cīt̰ aēibiiō vahištā yōi zrazdā̊° aŋhən mazdāi

31,2. yezī āiš nōit̰ uruuānē aduuā̊ aibī.dərəštā vax́iiā̊
at̰ vā̊ vīspə̄ṇg āiiōi yaϑā ratūm ahurō vaēdā
mazdā̊ aiiā̊ ąsaiiā̊ yā aṣ̌āt̰ hacā juuāmahī

31,3. yąm dā̊ mainiiū āϑrācā aṣ̌ācā cōiš rānōibiiā xšnūtəm
hiiat̰ uruuatəm cazdōŋhuuadəbiiō° tat̰ nə̄ mazdā vīduuanōi vaocā
hizuuā ϑβahiiā ā̊ŋhō yā juuaṇtō vīspə̄ṇg vāuraiiā

31,4. yadā aṣ̌əm zəuuīm aŋhən mazdā̊scā ahurā̊ŋhō
aṣ̌icā ārmaitī vahištā išasā manaŋhā
maibiiō xšaϑrəm aojōŋhuuat̰° yehiiā vərədā vanaēmā drujəm

31,5. tat̰ mōi vīcidiiāi vaocā hiiat̰ mōi aṣ̌ā dātā vahiiō
vīduiiē vohū manaŋhā mə̄ṇcā daidiiāi yehiiā mā ərəšiš
tācīt̰ mazdā ahurā yā nōit̰ vā aŋhat̰ aŋhaitī vā

31,6. ahmāi aŋhat̰ vahištəm yə̄ mōi vīduuā̊ vaocāt̰ haiϑīm
mąϑrəm yim hauruuatātō aṣ̌ahiiā amərətātascā
mazdāi auuat̰ xšaϑrəm hiiat̰ hōi vohū vaxšat̰ manaŋhā

31,7. yastā maṇtā pouruiiō raocə̄bīš rōiϑβən xᵛāϑrā
huuō xraϑβā dąmiš aṣ̌əm yā dāraiiat̰ vahištəm manō
tā mazdā mainiiū uxšiiō yə̄ ā nūrə̄mcīt̰ ahurā hāmō

31,8. at̰ ϑβā mə̄ŋ́hī° pouruuīm mazdā yazūm[1] stōi manaŋhā
vaŋhə̄uš ptarə̄m[2] manaŋhō hiiat̰ ϑβā hə̄m cašmainī [həṇ]grabəm
haiϑīm aṣ̌ahiiā dąmīm aŋhə̄uṣ̌ ahurəm š́iiaoϑanaēšū

31,9. ϑβōi as ārmaitiš° ϑβə̄ ā gə̄uš tašā as xratuš[3]
mainiiə̄uš° mazdā ahurā hiiat̰ ax́iiāi dadā̊ paϑąm
vāstriiāt̰ vā āitē yə̄ vā nōit̰ aŋhat̰ vāstriiō

31,10. at̰ hī aiiā̊ frauuarətā vāstrīm ax́iiāi fšuiiaṇtəm
ahurəm aṣ̌auuanəm vaŋhə̄uš fšə̄ŋ́hīm° manaŋhō
nōit̰ mazdā auuāstriiō dauuąscinā humərətōiš baxštā

---

[1] yazūm, Geldner yezīm.
[2] ptarə̄m, Geldner patarə̄m.
[3] as xratuš, Geldner as xratūš, inexact for aš.xratuš?

Yasna 31. Tā-vē-urvātā Hāiti

31,1 Keeping in mind these rules of yours we pronounce words (as yet) unheard to those who by the rules of deceit destroy the possessions of truth, but (which are) best for those who are faithful to Mazdā.

31,2. If the way better to tread is not seen by the (faithful), then I approach you all since Mazdā Ahura knows the judgment on these two shares, (a judgment) through which we can live in accordance with truth.

31,3. (Tell us about) the gratification which you grant with (your) spirit and (your) fire and which you assign through truth, according to the balance, which is the rule for (determining the benefit of) the conscientious. Tell us about that with the tongue of your mouth, O Mazdā, so that (we) may know (it) and I, applying it, may win over all the living.

31,4. When Mazdā and the (other) Ahuras are present, as well as truth worthy of invocation, along with reward and right-mindedness, then with good thought I hope to gain for myself strong power through the increase of which we may defeat deceit.

31,5. Tell me about the better (part) which you have assigned to me through truth, that I may discern it and that I may learn through good thought from (Him) whose prophet (I am), and note in my mind which things will not be, and which will be, O Mazdā Ahura.

31,6. The best (part) shall be for Him, the Knowing one, who may pronounce for me the true manthra concerning integrity and immortality of truth. That power (shall be) for Mazdā which He shall make grow with His good thought.

31,7. The Primal one who conceived (the manthra): "Let the free spaces be filled with light," with His intellect created truth. By that spirit by which one upholds best thought you still grow, O Mazdā Ahura, you who (have remained) the same until today.[1]

31,8. Thus, when I grasp you with my eyes, O Mazdā, I realize that it is through (your) thought that you, the Primal one, are youthful, the father of good thought, the true creator of truth and the Ahura (judging) the deeds of the world.

31,9. Right-mindedness was yours, yours also was the most intellectual fashioner of the cow, O Mazdā Ahura, when by virtue of your spirit you opened ways for her, so that she could join either the herdsman or whoever might not be a herdsman.

31,10. Of these two (the cow) chose for herself the cattle-breeding herdsman as a truthful master, the bondsman of good thought. The non-herdsman, O Mazdā, does not enjoy a good reputation, however much he may shout.

---

[1] Stanzas 31,7-8 describe the miraculous nature of Ahura Mazdā who is primal, creator, father, and judge and, simultaneously, youthful and still growing and who is still today one and the same.

31,11. hiiaṯ nə̄ mazdā paouruuīm gaēϑåscā tašō daēnåscā
ϑβā manaŋhā xratūšcā hiiaṯ astuuaṇtəm dadå uštanəm
hiiaṯ š́iiaoϑanācā sə̄ṇghąscā yaϑrā varənə̄ṇg vaså dāiietē

31,12. aϑrā vācəm baraitī miϑahuuacå vā ərəš.vacå° vā
vīduuå vā əuuīduuå vā ahiiā zərədācā manaŋhācā
ānuš.haxš ārmaitiš° mainiiū pərəsaitē[1] yaϑrā maēϑā

31,13. yā frasā auuīšiiā yā vā mazdā pərəsaētē[2] taiiā
yə̄ vā kasə̄uš aēnaŋhō ā mazištąm [a]iiamaitē būjəm
tā cašmə̄ṇg ϑβisrā hārō aibī aṣ̌ā [aibī.]vaēnahī vīspā

31,14. tā ϑβā pərəsā ahurā yā zī āitī jə̄ṇghaticā
yå išudō dadəṇtē dāϑranąm hacā aṣ̌aonō
yåscā mazdā drəguuō.dəbiiō° yaϑā tå aŋhən hə̄ṇkərətā hiiaṯ

31,15. pərəsā auuaṯ yā maēniš[3] yə̄ drəguuāitē xšaϑrəm hunāitī
duš.š́iiaoϑanāi ahurā yə̄ nōiṯ jiiōtūm hanarə vīnastī
vāstriiehiiā aēnaŋhō pasə̄uš vīrāatcā adrujiiaṇtō

31,16. pərəsā auuaṯ yaϑā huuō yə̄ hudānuš dəm‹ā›nahiia[4] xšaϑrəm
šōiϑrahiiā vā daxiiə̄uš vā aṣ̌ā fradaϑāi aspərəzatā
ϑβāuuąs mazdā ahurā yadā huuō aŋhaṯ yā.š́iiaoϑanascā

31,17. katārəm aṣ̌auuā vā drəguuå vā vərənauuaitē[5] maziiō
vīduuå vīdušē mraotū mā əuuīduuå aipī də̄bāuuaiiaṯ
zdī nə̄ mazdā ahurā vaŋhə̄uš fradaxštā manaŋhō

31,18. mā.ciš aṯ və̄ drəguuatō mąϑrąscā gūštā sāsnåscā
āzī[6] dəmānəm vīsəm vā šōiϑrəm vā daxiiūm vā [ā]dāṯ
dušitācā marəkaēcā° aϑā īš sāzdūm snaiϑišā

31,19. gūštā yə̄ maṇtā aṣ̌əm ahūm.biš° vīduuå ahurā
ərəžuxδāi vacaŋhąm xšaiiamnō hizuuō vasō
ϑβā āϑrā suxrā mazdā vaŋhāu vīdātā rąnaiiå

31,20. yə̄ āiiaṯ aṣ̌auuanəm diuuamnəm hōi aparəm xšiiō
darəgə̄m āiiū təmaŋhō duš.xᵛarəϑəm° auuaētās vacō
təm vå[7] ahūm drəguuaṇtō š́iiaoϑanāiš xᵛāiš daēnā naēšaṯ

[1] pərəsaitē, Geldner pərəsāitē.
[2] pərəsaētē, Geldner pərəsāitē.
[3] maēniš, Geldner mainiš.
[4] dəm‹ā›nahiiā, Geldner dəmanahiiā, many mss. dəmnahiiā.
[5] vərənauuaitē, Geldner vərənuuaitē.
[6] āzī, i.e. ā-zī.
[7] vå, Geldner vā.

31,11. Since, O Mazdā, with your thought you fashioned for us what is the first, the possessions and the religious views, as well as the intellects, when you created material life, when (you created) the actions and words where the wisher makes use of his preferences —

31,12. where there is doubt[1] as to whether it is a man of false words or one of true words, a knowing one or an ignorant one who, following his heart and thought raises his voice there, then (one's) right-mindedness shall take counsel with (his) spirit.

31,13. Through truth you see all things, O Mazdā, perceiving them with the gleam of your eye(s), be it two persons taking open counsel with each other, or be it in secret, or be it a person who, being guilty of just a small injury, shall incur the greatest punishment.

31,14. I ask you, O Mazdā Ahura, about the things that are approaching and will reach (us), about the invigorating gifts people will obtain from the truthful one or from the deceitful, and how they will be there when the reckoning (takes place).

31,15. I ask you, O Ahura, about the punishment for the evil-doer who delegates power to the deceitful one and who does not find a livelihood without injury to the cattle and men of the undeceiving herdsman.

31,16. I ask you, O Mazdā Ahura, about that generous person, one such as you, who, with truth, strives to promote the power over house, county, and land: How and when will he be present, and with what actions?

31,17. Is the truthful one more convincing or the deceitful one? Let the knowing one speak to the Knowing one. Let the ignorant one henceforth not delude (people). Be the teacher of good thought to us, O Mazdā Ahura.

31,18. Let no (adherent) of the deceitful one listen to your manthras and teachings. For he renders house, village, county, and land uninhabitable and ruined. Teach them therefore with your weapon.

31,19. The healer of existence, the knowing one who conceives truth, has listened (to your teachings). At will he is in control of his tongue for the sake of the correct uttering of the words, at the distribution of the balances in the good (way)[2] with your red fire, O Mazdā Ahura.

31,20. Brilliant things instead of weeping will be (the reward) for the person who comes to the truthful one. But a long period of darkness, foul food, and the word 'woe' — to such an existence your religious view will lead you, O deceitful ones, because of your own actions.[3]

---

[1] 'where there is doubt': uncertain.

[2] 'in the good (way)', or: 'at the good (reward to be distributed)'.

[3] 'your religious view ... because of your own actions': The use of the possessive pronoun xᵛa 'own' stresses the paradox that the deceitful themselves are guilty of their misfortune, cf. 46,5.11, 51,13-14.

31,21. mazdå dadāt̰ ahurō hauruuatō amərətātascā
būrōiš ā aṣ̌aχiiācā xᵛāpaiϑiiāt̰ xšaϑrahiiā sarō
vaŋhəuš vazduuarə̄ manaŋhō yə̄ hōi mainiiū šiiaoϑanāišcā uruuaϑō

31,22. ciϑrā ī hudåŋhē yaϑənā[1] vaēdəmnāi manaŋhā
vohū huuō xšaϑrā aṣ̌əm vacaŋhā šiiaoϑanācā haptī
huuō tōi mazdā ahurā vāzištō aŋhaitī astiš

End of Yasna 31

[1] yaϑənā, Geldner yaϑanā.

31,21. From His own wide shelter of integrity and immortality, of truth and power, Mazdā Ahura gives the fruit of good thought (to the person) who is His ally in spirit and actions.

31,22. Bright things are (in store) for the munificent one, who already possesses them in his thought. Through good power he holds truth in word and in action. He shall be your most welcome guest, O Mazdā Ahura.

End of Yasna 31

Yasna 32. Xᵛaētumaitī Hāiti

32,1. Axiiācā xᵛaētuš yāsat̰ ahiiā vərəzə̄nəm mat̰ airiiamnā
ahiiā daēuuā mahmī manōi ahurahiiā uruuāzəmā mazdā̊
ϑβōi dūtā̊ŋhō ā̊ŋhāmā tə̄ṇg dāraiiō yōi vā̊ daibišəṇtī

32,2. aēibiiō mazdā̊ ahurō sārəmnō vohū manaŋhā
xšaϑrāt̰ hacā paitī.mraot̰ aṣ̌ā huš.haxā xᵛə̄nuuātā
spəṇtąm və̄ ārmaitīm vaŋᵛhīm° varəmaidī hā nə̄ aŋhat̰

32,3. at̰ yūš daēuuā vīspā̊ŋhō akāt̰ manaŋhō stā ciϑrəm
yascā vā̊ maš yazaitē drūjascā pairimatōišcā
šiiaomąm aipī daibitānā yāiš asrūdūm[1] būmiiā̊ haptaiϑē

32,4. yāt̰[2] yūštā framīmaϑā yā maṣ̌iiā acištā daṇtō
vaxšəṇtē daēuuō.zuštā vaŋhə̄uš sīždiiamnā manaŋhō
mazdā̊ ahurahiiā xratə̄uš nasiiaṇtō aṣ̌āatcā

32,5. tā dəbənaōtā maṣ̌īm hujiiātōiš amərətātascā
hiiat̰ vā̊ akā manaŋhā yə̄ṇg daēuuə̄ṇg akascā mainiiuš
akā šiiaoϑanəm vacaŋhā yā fracinas drəguuaṇtəm xšaiiō[3]

32,6. pourū[4] aēnā̊ ə̄nāxštā yāiš srāuahiieitī yezī tāiš aϑā
hātā.marānē ahurā vahištā vōistā manaŋhā
ϑβahmī və̄ mazdā xšaϑrōi aṣ̌āicā sə̄ṇghō vīdąm

32,7. aēšąm aēnaŋhąm naēcīt̰ vīduuā̊ aojōi hādrōiiā
yā jōiiā sə̄ṇghaitē yāiš srāuuī xᵛaēnā aiiaŋhā
yaēšąm tū ahurā irixtəm mazdā vaēdištō ahī

32,8. aēšąm aēnaŋhąm vīuuaŋhušō srāuuī yimascīt̰
yə̄ maṣ̌iiə̄ṇg cixšnušō ahmākə̄ṇg gāuš bagā xᵛārəmnō
aēšąmcīt̰ ā ahmī ϑβahmī vīciϑōi aipī

32,9. duš.sastiš srauuā̊ mōrəṇdat̰ huuō jiiātə̄uš sə̄ṇghanāiš xratūm
apō mā īštīm [apa]iiaṇtā bərəxδąm hāitīm vaŋhə̄uš manaŋhō
tā uxδā mainiiə̄uš° mahiiā mazdā aṣ̌āicā yūšmaibiiā gərəzē

32,10. huuō mā nā srauuā̊ mōrəṇdat̰ yə̄ acištəm vaēnaŋhē° aogədā
gąm ašibiiā huuarəcā yascā dāϑə̄ṇg drəguuatō dadāt̰
yascā vāstrā vīuuāpat̰ yascā vadarə̄ vōiždat̰ aṣ̌āunē

[1] asrūdūm, Geldner asrūždūm.
[2] yāt̰, var. yāat̰.
[3] xšaiiō, var. xšiiō.
[4] pourū, most mss. have pouru.

Yasna 32. Khwaētumaitī Hāiti

32,1. In my recital, O Daēvas, the family and the community along with the tribe ask for His, Mazdā Ahura's, favor[1] (by praying): "Let us be your people. You scatter those who are hostile to you."

32,2. Mazdā Ahura, being associated with good thought and being a good friend of sun-like truth, answers them by virtue of His power: "We choose your holy and good right-mindedness. Let it be ours!"

32,3. But all you Daēvas are seed of evil thought, as is the 'great' person worshipping you, as well as the actions of deceit and contempt, for which again and again you have become notorious in the seventh clime of the Earth[2] —

32,4. since you, (the Daēvas), order the worst things, by producing which the mortals hope to prosper as your minions, flinching from good thought and straying away from the intellect of Mazdā Ahura and from truth.

32,5. You (Daēvas) cheat the mortals of good life and immortality in the same way as both the evil spirit, (associated) with evil thought, (cheated) you, the Daēvas, and the action (inspired) by evil word, by which a ruler recognizes a deceitful person.

32,6. Through best thought, O Mazdā Ahura, you know of the many peace-breaking crimes by which the deceitful one strives for fame. You who remember people's merits and demerits, let praise for you and for truth be spread in your realm.

32,7. I sincerely declare I have no knowledge of such crimes which are praised by the violent one,[3] for which one is interrogated with the glowing metal and of which you, O Mazdā Ahura, know best the outcome.

32,8. Even Yima, the son of Vivahvan, became notorious for such crimes. He, wishing to gratify the mortals, our people, failed by calling himself God.[4] As for me, in regard to such (crimes) I submit to your decision,[5] O Mazdā.

32,9. The blasphemer, by his commandeerings, spoils (our) reputation and the intellect of livelihood. He robs (us) of the authority esteemed by good thought. With these utterances of my spirit I complain to you, O Mazdā, and to truth.

32,10. That man spoils (our) reputation who professes what is the worst in order to see the cow and the sun with his eyes, who makes the just subject to the deceitful one and ravages the pastures and brandishes his weapon against the truthful one

[1] Here and in the following stanzas Zarathushtra mocks and derides the Daēvas who have come in order to grab the offerings made by the truthful.
[2] 'the seventh clime of the Earth', the clime Khvaniratha, is the central of the seven parts of the world.
[3] 'crimes praised by the violent one': uncertain.
[4] Yima (Yima Khshaēta, Persian Jamshīd) was guilty of a lie which caused the loss of paradise.
[5] 'I submit to your decision': uncertain.

32,11. taēcīṯ mā mōrəṇdən jiiōtūm yōi drəguuaṇtō[1] mazbīš[2] cikōitərəš
aŋᵛhīšcā° aŋhauuascā[3] apaiieitī raēxənaŋhō vaēdəm
yōi vahištāṯ ašaono[4] mazdā rārəšiiąn manaŋhō

32,12. yā rā̊ŋhaiiən srauuaŋhā vahištāṯ śiiaoϑanāṯ marətānō
aēibiiō mazdā̊ akā mraoṯ yōi gəuš uruuāxš.uxtī mōrəṇdən jiiōtūm
yāiš grəhmā° a̰šāṯ varatā karapā xšaϑrəmcā īšanąm drujəm

32,13. yā xšaϑrā grəhmō° hīšasaṯ acištahiiā dəmānē manaŋhō
aŋhəuš marəxtārō[5] ahiiā yaēcā mazdā jīgərəzaṯ kāmē
ϑβahiiā mąϑrānō dūtəm[6] yə̄ īš pāṯ darəsāṯ a̰šahiiā

32,14. ahiiā grəhmō° ā.hōiϑōi nī kāuuaiiascīṯ xratūš [nī.]dadaṯ
varəcā.hīcā[7] fraidiuuā hiiaṯ vīsəṇtā drəguuaṇtəm auuō
hiiaṯcā gāuš jaidiiāi mraoī yə̄ dūraošəm saocaiiaṯ auuō

32,15. anāiš ā vī.nənāsā yā karapō.tā̊scā° kəuuītā̊scā
auuāiš aibī yə̄ṇg daiṇtī nōiṯ jiiātəuš xšaiiamnə̄ṇg vasō
tōi ābiiā bairiiā̊ṇtē vaŋhəuš ā dəmānē manaŋhō

32,16. haməm taṯ vahištācīṯ yə̄ ušuruiiē siiascīṯ[8] dahmahiiā
xšaiiąs mazdā ahurā yehiiā mā aiϑīšcīṯ duuaēϑā
hiiaṯ aēnańhe° drəguuatō əəānū išiiə̄ṇg aŋhaiiā

End of Yasna 32

---

[1] drəguuaṇtō, Geldner drəguuatō.
[2] mazbīš, Geldner mazibīš.
[3] aŋhauuascā, Geldner aŋhuuascā.
[4] a̰šaonō, Geldner a̰šāunō.
[5] marəxtārō, Geldner maraxtārō.
[6] dūtəm, Geldner dūtīm.
[7] varəcā.hīcā, Geldner varəcā̊ hīcā.
[8] siiascīṯ, var. saiiascīṯ.

32,11. Indeed, those deceitful 'ladies and lords' spoil (our) livelihood, who 'distinguish' themselves with 'great deeds': robbing (people) of the possession of their heritage — and who rip the truthful away from best thought, O Mazdā.

32,12. Mazdā speaks condemning words to those who, by (their) speech, make the mortals fall away from the best action, and who spoil the life of the cow by saying "move on".[1] On their account the Karapan chooses Grehma practices as well as the power of the promoters of deceit, rather than truth.

32,13. Through that power the Grehma gang, destroyers of this world, wishes to sit down in the house of worst thought, O Mazdā. In their (wicked) desire, they complain about the people of your manthra-keeper preventing them from seeing truth.

32,14. The Kavis, being a Grehma gang, lay their intellects and their dignities into its fetter[2] day by day. They take their positions (at the sacrifice) in order to assist the deceitful one and, (by obeying) the command[3] "let the (sacrificial) animal be killed," to assist the one who inflames[4] the 'fire-resisting' (Haoma Dūraosha).[5]

32,15. Owing to such (activities) Karapanship and Kaviship are lost, being the outcome of (the activities of the truthful ones) whom they want to harness and make lose control over their lives. The (truthful) will be cared for by those two, (integrity and immortality), in the house of good thought.

32,16. O Mazdā Ahura, (it is you) who have power over any pious man lying in distress and whose fear frightens him: that equals the very best which, (contrary) to the crime of the deceitful one, is seen following behind the invigorators.[6]

End of Yasna 32

[1] 'move on' is, perhaps, an evil spell spoken by the deceitful to the cow, or to the soul of the cow, at the moment of slaughtering the animal.

[2] 'its fetter', i.e. the fetter of truth, or rather: the fetter of Haoma Dūraosha?

[3] '(by obeying) the command': uncertain.

[4] The pun 'the one who inflames the fire-resisting (Haoma)' denotes a a deceitful priest who performs a certain Haoma rite considered unlawful by Zarathushtra.

[5] The etymological meaning of Dūraosha (dūraoša), which in the Younger Avesta is an epithet of the Haoma, the intoxicant ritual drink of the Iranians, is 'fire-resisting, resisting annihilation'. In the Younger Avesta it is understood as 'preventing death, providing immortality'. Zarathushtra polemizes against the use of Haoma or, at least, against its misuse (cf. 48,10).

[6] 'the very best ... following behind the invigorators', i.e. the gifts brought by the pious people.

Yasna 33. Yaϑāišiϑā Hāiti

33,1. Yaϑā āiš[1] iϑā varəšaitē yā dātā aŋhəuš paouruiiehiiā
ratū[š][2] šiiaoϑanā razištā drəguuataēcā hiiatcā ašāunē
yexiiācā hə̄miiāsaitē[3] miϑahiiā yācā hōi ārəzuuā

33,2. at̰ yə̄ akəm drəguuāitē vacaŋhā vā at̰ vā manaŋhā
zastōibiiā vā varəšaitī vaŋhāu vā cōiϑaitē astīm
tōi vārāi rādəṇtī ahurahiiā zaošē mazdā̊

33,3. yə̄ ašāunē vahištō xᵛaētū vā at̰ vā vərəzə̄niiō
airiiamnā vā ahurā vīdąs vā ϑβaxšaŋhā gauuōi
at̰ huuō ašahiiā aŋhat̰ vaŋhə̄uscā vāstrē manaŋhō

33,4. yə̄ ϑβat̰ mazdā asruštīm akəmcā manō yazāi apā
xᵛaētə̄uscā tarə̄.maitīm vərəzə̄naxiiācā nazdištąm drujəm
airiiamnascā° nadəṇtō gə̄uscā vāstrāt̰ acištəm mantūm

33,5. yastē vīspə̄.maziš̌təm səraošəm zbaiiā auuaŋhānē
apānō darəgō.jiiāitīm ā xšaϑrəm vaŋhə̄uš manaŋhō
ašāt̰ ā ərəzūš paϑō yaēšū mazdā̊ ahurō šaēitī°

33,6. yə̄ zaotā ašā ərəzuš° huuō mainiiə̄uš° ā vahištāt̰ kaiiā
ahmāt̰ auuā manaŋhā yā vərəziieidiiāi maṇtā vāstriiā
tā tōi iziiā[4] ahurā mazdā darštōišcā hə̄m.parštōišcā

33,7. ā mā [ā]idūm vahištā ā xᵛaiϑiiācā mazda darəšatcā
ašā vohū manaŋhā yā sruiiē parə̄ magaonō[5]
āuuiš nā̊ aṇtarə hə̄ṇtū nəmaxᵛaitīš ciϑrā̊ rātaiiō

33,8. frō mōi [fra]uuōizdūm arəϑā tā yā vohū šiiauuāi manaŋhā
yasnəm mazdā xšmāuuatō at̰ vā ašā staomiiā vacā̊
dātā və̄ amərətā̊scā utaiiūitī hauruuatās draonō

33,9. at̰ tōi mazdā təm mainiiūm ašaoxšaiiaṇtā̊[6] sarəidiiaiiā̊°
xᵛāϑrā maeϑā maiiā vahištā barətū manaŋhā
aiiā̊ ārōi hākurənəm yaiiā̊ haciṇtē uruuąno

---

[1] yaϑa aiš, Geldner yaϑaiš.
[2] ratūš šiiaoϑanā for ratū šiiaoϑanā owing to erroneous segmentation of spoken text.
[3] hə̄miiāsaitē, Geldner həməmiiāsaitē.
[4] iziiā, Geldner iziiāi.
[5] magaonō, Geldner magāunō.
[6] ašaoxšaiiaṇtā̊, var. ašaoxšiiaṇtā̊.

Yasna 33. Yathāish-ithā Hāiti

33,1. Just as by those (present), so the straightest actions following the laws of the first existence, shall be performed by the judge both for the deceitful one and the truthful one, as well as for the one whose wrong and right (deeds) are reckoned together.

33,2. The person who works evil for the deceitful one by his word, his thought, or his hands, or (the one who) wins him over to be his guest at the good (reward),[1] all these heed His will, (abiding) in the pleasure of Mazdā Ahura.

33,3. The person who is best to the truthful one, by family, being a member of the same community, by tribe, O Ahura, or by caring zealously for the cow, that person will be in the pasture of truth and good thought.

33,4. By praying, I will turn disobedience and evil thought away from you, O Mazdā, as well as the scorn of the family and the deceit closest to the community and (your) revilers in the tribe, and I will turn the worst counsel from the pasture of the cow.

33,5. At the resting-place I shall invoke your utmost attention, having reached long life and the power of good thought and the paths straight through truth, whereon Mazdā Ahura dwells.

33,6. As a leading priest straightforward in truth, in accordance with the best spirit I am pleased with the thought with which one thinks pastoral works should be performed. With that (thought) I implore your sight and your counsel, O Mazdā Ahura.

33,7. Come hither to me, you Best ones, boldly and in persons, O Mazdā, with truth, and with good thought for which I am heard far beyond the faithful offerers. Let bright reverential gifts be manifest among us.

33,8. Take heed of these matters of mine which I will pursue with good thought: worship for one such as you, O Mazdā, and words full of praise through truth. Integrity and immortality are offered to you with stability, as oblation.

33,9. O Mazdā, with best thought let one bring to you through the free space facing me[2] that spirit of the two rivals[3] who make truth grow. The fellowship of these two whose souls are in agreement has been apportioned.

[1] 'at the good (reward)', or: 'in (his) estate'?
[2] 'through the free space facing me': uncertain.
[3] 'the two rivals': uncertain.

33,10. vīspā̊ stōi hujītaiiō   yā̊ zī ā̊ŋharə̄ yā̊scā həṇtī
yā̊scā mazdā bauuaiṇtī[1]   ϑβahmī hīš zaošē ābaxšō.huuā°
vohū uxšiiā manaŋhā   xšaϑrā aṣ̌ācā uštā tanūm

33,11. yə̄ səuuištō ahurō   mazdā̊scā ārmaitišcā
aṣ̌əmcā frādaṯ.gaēϑəm   manascā vohū xšaϑrəmcā
sraotā mōi mərəždātā mōi   ādāi kahiiācīṯ[2] paitī

33,12. us mōi [uz]ārəšuuā ahurā   ārmaitī təuuīšīm dasuuā
spə̄ništā mainiiū mazdā   vaŋhuiiā zauuō ādā
aṣ̌ā hazō ə̄mauuaṯ   vohū manaŋhā fsəratūm°

33,13. rafəδrāi vourucašānē   dōišī mōi yā və̄ abifrā
tā xšaϑrahiiā ahurā   yā vaŋhə̄uš aṣ̌iš manaŋhō
frō spəṇtā ārmaitē   aṣ̌ā daēnā̊ [fra]daxšaiiā

33,14. aṯ rātąm zaraϑuštrō   tanuuascīṯ xᵛax́iiā̊ uštanəm
dadāitī pauruuatātəm   manaŋhascā vaŋhə̄uš mazdāi
šiiaoϑanahiiā aṣ̌ā[3] yācā   uxδax́iiācā səraošəm xšaϑrəmcā

End of Yasna 33

[1] bauuaiṇtī, var. buuaiṇtī.
[2] kahiiācīṯ, Geldner kahiiāicīṯ.
[3] aṣ̌ā, Geldner aṣ̌āi.

33,10. Receive, O Mazdā, in your approval all good gains which have existed, exist, and will exist. Grow at will in your body through good thought, power, and truth.

33,11. (You who are) the strongest and the wise(st) Ahura,[1] and (you who are) right-mindedness, truth furthering the possessions, good thought, and power, listen to me. Have mercy on me at any apportionment.

33,12. Rise up to me, O Mazdā Ahura. Take strength through right-mindedness and the most holy spirit, swiftness through good apportionment, forceful superiority through truth, and joy through good thought.[2]

33,13. For support, O far-seeing Ahura, show me those characteristics of your power, which are a reward of good thought. O holy right-mindedness, teach (us) the religious views through truth.

33,14. To Mazdā, Zarathushtra offers as a gift even the life force of his own body, the first offering of good thought as well as that of the action (performed) with truth, and (he offers his) obedience to the (divine) utterance and his power.

End of Yasna 33

---

[1] Mazdā, lit. 'wise', is coordinated here with the adj. 'strongest', thus having the function of an adjectival attribute.

[2] 'take strength etc.': Ahura Mazdā is invited to enjoy the offerings of the pious, both spiritual and material, in order to restore his power, cf. 34,1.

Yasna 34. Yā.šiiaoϑanā Hāiti

34,1. yā šiiaoϑanā yā vacaŋhā yā yasnā amərətatātəm
aṣ̌əmcā taibiiō[1] dåŋhā mazdā xšaϑrəmcā hauruuatātō
aēšąm tōi ahurā əhmā pourutəmāiš dastē

34,2. atcā ī tōi manaŋhā mainiiəuščā° vaŋhəuš[2] vīspā dātā
spəṇtaxiiācā nərəš šiiaoϑanā yehiiā uruuā aṣ̌ā hacaitē
pairigaēϑē xšmāuuatō vahmē mazdā garōbiš° stūtąm

34,3. at̰ tōi miiazdəm ahurā nəmaŋhā aṣ̌āicā dāmā
gaēϑå vīspå ā xšaϑrōi yå[3] vohū ϑraoštā manaŋhā
ārōi zī hudåŋhō vīspāiš mazdā xšmāuuasū sauuō

34,4. at̰ tōi ātrəm ahurā aojōŋhuuaṇtəm aṣ̌ā usəmahī
asīštīm[4] əmauuaṇtəm stōi rapaṇtē ciϑrā.auuaŋhəm
at̰ mazdā daibišiiaṇtē zastāištāiš dərəštā.aēnaŋhəm

34,5. kat̰ və xšaϑrəm kā īštiš° šiiaoϑanāi mazdā yaϑā vā hahmī
aṣ̌ā vohū manaŋhā ϑrāiiōidiiāi drigūm yūšmākəm
parə vå vīspāiš [parə.]vaoxəmā daēuuāišcā xrafstrāiš maṣ̌iiāišcā

34,6. yezī aϑā stā haiϑīm mazdā aṣ̌ā vohū manaŋhā
at̰ tat̰ mōi daxštəm dātā ahiiā aŋhəuš vīspā maēϑā
yaϑā vå yazəmnascā uruuāidiiå stauuas aiienī paitī

34,7. kuϑrā tōi arədrā mazdā yōi vaŋhəuš vaēdənā manaŋhō
səṇghūš raēxənå aspəṇcīt̰ sādrācīt̰ caxraiiō ušəurū
naēcīm təm aniiəm yūšmat̰ vaēdā aṣ̌ā aϑā nå ϑrāzdūm

34,8. tāiš zī nå šiiaoϑanāiš biieṇtē yaēšū as pairī pourubiiō iϑiiejō
hiiat̰ as aojå[5] nāidiiåŋhəm ϑβahiiā mazdā ąstā uruuātahiiā
yōi nōit̰ aṣ̌əm mainiiaṇtā aēibiiō dūirē vohū as manō

34,9. yōi spəṇtąm ārmaitīm ϑβahiiā mazdā bərəxδąm vīdušō
duš.šiiaoϑanā auuazazat̰ vaŋhəuš əuuistī manaŋhō
aēibiiō maš aṣ̌ā siiazdat̰ yauuat̰ ahmat̰ aurunā xrafstrā

34,10. ahiiā vaŋhəuš manaŋhō šiiaoϑanā vaocat̰ gərəbąm huxratuš
spəṇtąmcā ārmaitīm dąmīm vīduuå hiϑąm aṣ̌ahiiā
tācā vīspā ahurā ϑβahmī mazdā xšaϑrōi ā vōiiaϑrā

---

1 taibiiō, Geldner taēibiiō.
2 mainiiəušcā vaŋhəuš, Geldner mainiiušcā vaŋhuš.
3 yå, var. yā.
4 asīštīm, var. asīštəm.
5 as aojå, Geldner as aojiiå, blunder for aš.aojå?

Yasna 34. Yā-shyaothanā Hāiti

34,1. The action, word, and worship through which you acquire immortality, truth, and the power of integrity, O Mazdā Ahura, (a share) of these is offered to you by us who are present in large numbers.[1]

34,2. All of the good spirit is offered to you thoughtfully, as well as the actions of the holy man whose soul is in harmony with truth, O Mazdā, at the glorification of one such as you, entrusting (our) possessions (to you) with songs of praises.

34,3. In reverence for you, O Mazdā Ahura, and for truth, we place in your power, as an offering to you, all (our) possessions, which you have nourished with good thought. For benefit has been apportioned by all among those such as you, O Munificent ones.

34,4. O Mazdā Ahura, we desire your fire, strong through truth, most vigorous and impetuous, to be of clear help to (your) supporter, but of visible injury to (your) enemy by the (recompenses) coming from its hands.

34,5. What is your power, what your command, O Mazdā, that may protect me, your poor dependent, with truth and good thought, at work as well as when I sleep? We have declared you to be superior to all Daēvas, beasts, and (evil) mortals.[2]

34,6. If this is the way you really are, O Mazdā, with truth and good thought, then make that clear to me all days of my life, so that I may come to you again, worshipping and praising you ever more joyously.

34,7. Where are those zestful persons, O Mazdā, who by knowledge of the bequests and legacies of good thought remove any misfortune and distress? In truth, I do not know any other than you. So protect us.

34,8. The multitude (of deceitful) fears us on account of those actions by which you send danger around them, when the strong one hits the weaker one, by the severity of your rule, O Mazdā. You send good thought far away from those who do not respect truth.

34,9. Through ignorance of good thought the evil-doers let holy right-mindedness esteemed by your knowing one go away, O Mazdā. Let a great (leader) keep truths[3] away from them, as far as (he shall keep) the fierce beasts away from us.

34,10. The person of good intellect speaks of grasping the actions of good thought, as well as (of grasping) holy right-mindedness, knowing it, the creative partner of truth, and (of) all those means of protection (found) in your power, O Mazdā.

---

[1] By enjoying the spiritual and material offerings presented to Him by the pious, Ahura Mazdā restores His power which will enable Him to win the decisive victory against the powers of darkness.
[2] 'to all Daēvas, beasts, and (evil) mortals', or: 'to all beasts: Daēvas and (evil) mortals'?
[3] The plural of 'truth' is also found in 49,1.

34,11. at̰ tōi ubē hauruuā̊scā xᵛarəϑāi.ā amərətatā̊scā
vaŋhəuš xšaϑrā manaŋhō aṣ̌ā mat̰ ārmaitiš vaxšt
utaiiūitī təuuīšī tāiš ā mazdā vīduuaēšąm ϑβōi.ahī[1]

34,12. kat̰ tōi rāzarə kat̰ vašī kat̰ vā stūtō kat̰ vā yasnahiiā
srūidiiāi mazdā frāuuaocā yā vīdāiiāt̰ aṣ̌īš rāšnąm
sīšā nā̊ aṣ̌ā paϑō vaŋhəuš xᵛaētəṇg manaŋhō

34,13. təm aduuānəm ahurā yəm mōi mraoš vaŋhəuš manaŋhō
daēnā̊ saošiiaṇtąm yā hū.kərətā[2] aṣ̌ācīt̰ uruuāxšat̰
hiiat̰ cəuuištā[3] hudā̊biio[4] mīždəm mazdā yehiiā tū daϑrəm

34,14. tat̰ zī mazdā vairīm astuuaitē uštānāi dātā
vaŋhəuš š́iiaoϑanā manaŋhō yōi zī gəuš vərəzānē aziiā̊
xšmākąm hucistīm ahurā xratəuš aṣ̌ā frādō vərəzə̄nā

34,15. mazdā at̰ mōi vahištā srauuā̊scā š́iiaoϑanācā vaocā
tā tū vohū manaŋhā aṣ̌ācā išudəm stūtō
xšmākā xšaϑrā ahurā fərašə̄m vasnā haiϑiiə̄m dā̊ ahūm

End of Yasna 34

---

[1] vīduuaēšąm ϑβōi.ahī, or: vīduuaēšąm.ϑβōi ahī?
[2] hū.kərətā, Geldner hū.karətā.
[3] cəuuištā, Geldner ciuuištā.
[4] hudā̊biiō, Geldner hudābiiō.

34,11. Both integrity and immortality serve you as food.[1] By the power of good thought, right-mindedness along with truth, make stability and strength grow. With all these you make the enemies tremble,[2] O Mazdā.

34,12. What is your directive? What do you wish? What praise and what worship? Proclaim so we can hear, O Mazdā, in what way one will distribute the reward for (obeying) your directives. Show us with truth the paths of good thought, easy to travel.

34,13. Show us that way which you have told me to be the way of good thought, the well-adorned way, on which the religious views of the benefactors proceed with truth itself toward the prize which you have accorded to the munificent ones and of which you are the award, O Mazdā Ahura.

34,14. For you, O Mazdā Ahura, grant this desirable possession to material life, through the action of good thought, you who are at the shelter of the fertile cow. (You grant) your good insight on account of the intellect which furthers (such) shelters through truth.

34,15. So tell me (which are) the best words and actions, (tell me) these with good thought, and tell me with truth (which is) the invigoration following the praise. Through your power, O Mazdā Ahura, make real the existence which is brilliant in value.

End of Yasna 34

[1] 'integrity and immortality' refer to the offerings of the pious as well as to the heavenly food with which these offerings are mystically identified.
[2] 'make the enemies tremble': uncertain.

Yasna 35-41. Yasna Haptaŋhāiti

Yasna 35

35,1. [Ahurəm mazdąm aṣ̌auuanəm aṣ̌ahe ratūm yazamaide. aməṣ̌ā spəṇtā huxšaϑrā huδā̊ŋhō yazamaide. vīspąm aṣ̌aonō stīm yazamaide mainiiəuuīmcā gaēϑiiąmcā bərəjā vaŋhəuš aṣ̌ahe bərəjā vaŋhuiiā̊ daēnaiiā̊ māzdaiiasnōiš.][1]

35,2. Humatanąm hūxtanąm huuarəštanąm° iiadacā aniiadacā vərəziiamnanąmcā vāuuərəzananąmcā mahī aibī.jarətārō naēnaēstārō yaϑənā[2] vohunąm mahī.

35,3. tat̰ at̰ vairimaidī[3] ahurā mazdā aṣ̌ā.srīrā hiiat̰ ī mainimadicā vaocōimācā varəzimācā[4] yā hātąm šiiaoϑananąm vahištā x́iiāt̰ ubōibiiā ahubiiā.

35,4. gauuōi adāiš tāiš šiiaoϑanāiš yāiš vahištāiš fraēšiiāmahī rāmācā vāstrəmcā dazdiiāi surunuuatascā asurunuuatascā xšaiiaṇtascā axšaiiaṇtascā.

35,5. huxšaϑrō.təmāi bāt̰[5] xšaϑrəm ahmat̰ hiiat̰ aibī dadəmahicā cīšmahicā huuąnmahicā hiiat̰ mazdāi ahurāi aṣ̌āicā hiiat̰ vahištāi.

35,6. yaϑā āt̰[6] utā nā vā nāirī vā vaēdā haiϑīm aϑā hat̰ vohū tat̰ əəādū vərəziiōtūcā īt̰ ahmāi fracā vātōiiōtū īt̰ aēibiiō yōi īt̰ aϑā vərəziiąn yaϑā īt̰ astī.

35,7. ahurahiiā at̰ zī at̰ vō mazdā̊ yasnəmcā vahməmcā vahištəm aməhmaidī gə̄uščā vāstrəm. tat̰ at̰ vō vərəziiāmahī fracā vātōiiāmahī yā.tə isāmaidē.

35,8. aṣ̌ahiiā āat̰ sairī aṣ̌ahiiā vərəzə̄ne kahmāicīt̰ hātąm jījišąm vahištąm ādā ubōibiiā ahubiiā.

35,9. imā āt̰ uxδā vacā̊ ahurā mazdā aṣ̌əm manaiiā[7] vahehiiā frauuaocāmā. ϑβąm at̰ aēšąm paitiiāstārəmcā fradaxštārəmcā dadəmaidē.

35,10. aṣ̌āatcā hacā vaŋhəuščā manaŋhō vaŋhəuščā xšaϑrāt̰ staotā-‹ā›iš[8] ϑβāt̰ ahurā staotōibiiō aibī uxδā ϑβāt̰ uxδōibiiō yasnā ϑβāt̰ yasnōibiiō.

---

[1] This section is a later addition.
[2] yaϑənā, Geldner yaϑanā.
[3] vairimaidī, Geldner vairīmaidī, Narten varəmaidī.
[4] varəzimācā Narten, Geldner vərəzimācā.
[5] bāt̰, var. bāat̰.
[6] yāt̰, var. yāat̰.
[7] manaiiā, Geldner maniiā.
[8] staotā-‹ā›iš for slightly incorrect staotāiš of the mss.

Yasna 35-41. Yasna Haptanghāiti

Yasna 35

35,1. [We worship Ahura Mazdā, the truthful judge of truth. We worship the Amesha Spentas, the munificent good rulers. We worship all the spiritual and material property of the truthful one with celebration of good truth, with celebration of the good Mazdayasnian Religion.]

35,2. We are the eulogists of the well-thought (thoughts), of the well-spoken (words), and of the well-performed (actions) that are being performed and that have been performed here and elsewhere, as we are also non-revilers of (all) good things.

35,3. O Ahura Mazdā, beautiful through truth, the following we would choose: that we might think, pronounce, and perform the actions that would be the best among the actions of the existing,[1] for both existences.

35,4. Through these best actions we urge those who listen as well as those who do not listen, those who hold power as well as those who do not hold power, to establish peace and (provide) a pasture for the cow.

35,5. Thus we offer, commit, and delegate the power which is with us to the best ruler, Mazdā Ahura, and to best truth.

35,6. Just as a man or a woman knows something (to be) true, being so, let him cultivate it for himself (as) a good seed grain, and let him make it known just as it is to those who would cultivate it.[2]

35,7. As we have realized worship and glorification of Ahura Mazdā to be best for you (all) and likewise the pasture of the cow, so we wish to cultivate it for you and make it known to the extent that we are able.

35,8. He has declared the best search for refuge for anyone among the existing to be in the shelter of truth and in the community of truth, for both existences.

35,9. O Ahura Mazdā, with a better devotion we wish to proclaim these uttered words as truth. We choose you to be their listener and elucidator.

35,10. In accordance with truth, good thought, and good power (we choose you) with a praise above praises, with an utterance above utterances, and with a worship above worships.

---

[1] 'the best among the actions of the existing (= of those who exist)', or: 'the best among the actions that are'.

[2] The section seems to deal with knowing and practicing a manthra.

Yasna 36

36,1. Ahiiā ϑβā āϑrō vərəzə̄nā paouruiiē pairijasāmaidē mazdā ahurā ϑβā ϑβā mainiiū spə̄ništā yə̄ ā axtiš ahmāi yə̄m axtōiiōi dåŋhē.

36,2. uruuāzišto huuō nå yātāiiā paitī.jamiiå ātarə mazdå ahurahiiā uruuāzištahiiā uruuāz‹a›iiā nąmištahiiā nəmaŋhā nå mazištāi yåŋhąm paitī.jamiiå.

36,3. ātarš vōi mazdå ahurahiiā ahī. mainiiuš vōi ahiiā spə̄ništō ahī. hiiat̰ vā tōi nāmanąm vāzištəm ātarə mazdå ahurahiiā tā ϑβā pairijasāmaidē.

36,4. vohū ϑβā manaŋhā vohū ϑβā aṣ̌ā vaŋhuiiå ϑβā cistōiš š́iiaoϑanāiščā vacə̄bīščā pairijasāmaidē.

36,5. nəmax́iiāmahī išūidiiāmahī ϑβā mazdā ahurā. vīspāiš ϑβā humatāiš vīspāiš hūxtāiš vīspāiš huuarəštāiš° pairijasāmaidē.

36,6. sraēštąm at̰ tōi kəhrpə̄m kəhrpąm āuuaēdaiiamahī mazdā ahurā imā raocå barəzištəm barəzəmanąm[1] auuat̰ yāt̰[2] huuarə auuācī.

Yasna 37

37,1. Iϑā āt̰ yazamaidē ahurəm mazdąm yə̄ gąmcā aṣ̌əmcā dāt̰ apascā dāt̰ uruuaråscā vaŋᵛhīš raocåscā dāt̰ būmīmcā vīspācā vohū.

37,2. ahiiā xšaϑrā mazə̄nācā hauuapaŋhāiščā tə̄m at̰ yasnanąm pauruuatātā yazamaidē yōi gə̄uš hacā š́iieiṇtī.

37,3. tə̄m at̰ āhūriiā nāmə̄nī mazdā.varā spəṇtō.təmā yazamaidē. tə̄m ahmākāiš azdəbīščā° uštānāiščā yazamaidē. [tə̄m aṣ̌aonąm[3] frauuaṣ̌īš narąmcā nāirinąmcā yazamaidē.][4]

37,4. aṣ̌əm at̰ vahištəm yazamaidē hiiat̰ sraēštəm hiiat̰ spəṇtəm hiiat̰ aməṣ̌əm hiiat̰ raocōŋhuuat̰° hiiat̰ vīspā vohū.

37,5. vohucā manō yazamaidē vohucā xšaϑrəm vaŋᵛhīmcā° daēnąm vaŋᵛhīmcā° fsəratūm vaŋᵛhīmcā° ārmaitīm.

---

[1] barəzəmanąm, Geldner barəzimanąm.
[2] yāt̰, var. yāat̰.
[3] aṣ̌aonąm, Geldner aṣ̌āunąm.
[4] The sentence in brackets seems to be a later addition.

Yasna 36

36,1. At first we approach you, O Mazdā Ahura, with the community of this fire[1], (we approach) you with your most holy spirit, you who are pain to the one whom you seize for painful treatment.

36,2. O fire of Mazdā Ahura, may you, the most delightful one, come to us for (your) share, may you come to us for the greatest of sharings, with the delight of the most delightful one, with the reverence of the most reverent one.

36,3. You are indeed the fire of Mazdā Ahura. You are indeed His most holy spirit. We approach you, O fire of Mazdā Ahura, (pronouncing) that of your names which is the most welcome among them.

36,4. We approach you with good thought, with good truth, and with the actions and words of good insight.

36,5. We worship and invigorate you, O Mazdā Ahura. We approach you with all our well-thought (thoughts), with all our well-spoken (words), with all our well-performed (actions).

36,6. We attribute to you, O Mazdā Ahura, the most beautiful body among bodies, these lights here[2] (as well as) yonder (light), the highest among the high since it was given the name 'sun'.[3]

Yasna 37

37,1. Herewith we worship Mazdā Ahura who created the cow and truth, who created the waters and the good plants, who created the lights and the earth and all good things.

37,2. For His power and greatness and artful works we worship Him with the pre-eminence of the worships of those who dwell in harmony with the cow.

37,3. Him we worship (by pronouncing) His Ahurian names dear to Mazdā and most holy. Him we worship with our bones and life force. [Him we worship (by mentioning) the Fravashis of the truthful men and women.]

37,4. We worship best truth, most beautiful, holy and immortal, full of light and containing all good things.

37,5. We worship good thought, good power, good religion, good joy, and good right-mindedness.

---

[1] 'with the community of this fire', or: 'with the shelter of this fire'?
[2] 'these lights here', i.e. the sacrificial fire.
[3] 'since it was given the name sun', i.e. since it was created by Ahura Mazdā.

Yasna 38

38,1. Imąm āat̰ ząm gənābīš haϑrā yazamaidē yā nå baraitī yåscā tōi gənå ahurā mazdā aṣ̌āt̰ hacā vairiiå tå yazamaidē:

38,2. īžå yaoštaiiō fəraštaiiō ārmataiio. vaŋᵛhīm° ābīš aṣ̌īm vaŋᵛhīm° īšəm vaŋᵛhīm° āzūitīm vaŋᵛhīm° frasastīm vaŋᵛhīm° parəṇdīm[1] yazamaidē.

38,3. apō at̰ yazamaidē maēkaiiaṇtīṣ̌cā[2] həbuuaiṇtīšcā frauuazaŋhō ahurānīš ahurahiiā hauuapaŋhā.[3] hupərəϑβåscā vå huuō.γžaϑåscā° hūšnāϑråscā ubōibiiā ahubiiā cagəmā.

38,4 ūitī yā və vaŋᵛhīš° ahurō mazdå nāmąn° dadāt̰ vaŋhudå hiiat̰ vå dadāt̰ tāiš vå yazamaidē tāiš friiąnmahī° tāiš nəmax́iiāmahī tāiš išūidiiāmahī.

38,5. apascā vå azīšcā vå mātərąšcā vå agəniiå drigudāiiaŋhō vīspō.pitīš[4] āuuaocāmā[5] vahištå sraēštå. auuā və vaŋᵛhīš° rātōiš darəgō.bāzāuš nāšū paitī viiādå paitī.səṇdå mātarō jītaiiō.

Yasna 39

39,1. Iϑā āt̰[6] yazamaidē gə̄uš uruuānəmcā tašānəmcā. ahmākə̄ṇg āat̰ urunō pasukanąmcā yōi nå jījišəṇtī yaēibiiascā tōi ā yaēcā aēibiio ā aŋhən.

39,2. daitikanąmcā aidiiūnąm hiiat̰ urunō yazamaidē. aṣ̌āunąm āat̰ urunō yazamaidē kudō.zātanąmcīt̰ narąmcā nāirinąmcā yaēšąm vahehīš daēnå vanaiṇtī vā və̄ṇghən vā vaonarə̄ vā.

39,3. āt̰[7] iϑā yazamaidē vaŋhūšcā īt̰ vaŋᵛhīšca° īt̰ spəṇtə̄ṇg aməṣ̌ə̄ṇg yauuaējiiō yauuaēsuuō yōi vaŋhə̄uš ā manaŋhō š́iieiṇtī yåscā ūitī.

39,4. yaϑā tū ī ahurā mazdā mə̄ṇghācā vaocascā dåscā varəšcā yā vohū aϑa tōi dadəmahī aϑā cīšmahī aϑā ϑβā āiš yazamaidē aϑā nəmax́iiāmahī aϑā išūidiiāmahī ϑβā mazdā ahurā.

39,5. vaŋhə̄uš xᵛaētə̄uš xᵛaētātā vaŋhə̄uš aṣ̌ahiiā ϑβā pairijasāmaidē vaŋhuiiå fsəratuuō° vaŋhuiiå ārmatōiš.

---

[1] parəṇdīm, var. pārəṇdīm.
[2] maēkaiiaṇtīšcā Narten, Geldner maēkaiṇtīšcā.
[3] hauuapaŋhā Narten, Geldner hauuapaŋhå.
[4] vīspō.pitīš Narten, Geldner vīspō.paitīš.
[5] āuuaocāmā Narten, Geldner auuaocāmā.
[6] āt̰, var. āat̰.
[7] āt̰, var. āat̰.

Yasna 38

38,1. We worship this earth that bears us. We worship it along with its women, and we worship those women who are yours, O Mazdā Ahura, worthy of being chosen in accordance with truth:

38,2. Abundances, purifications, brilliances, and right-mindednesses. And along with these we worship good reward, good invigoration, good nourishment, good praise, and good providence.[1]

38,3. We worship the waters which are tasty and juicy, the Ahurānīs which flow through the artful work of the Ahura. (We worship) you, (the waters) which provide good crossing, which flow well, and are good to swim in: a support for both existences.

38,4. Pronouncing the names which Mazdā Ahura, the Giver of the Good Things, gave you, O good ones, when He created you, we worship you with these (names), we appease you with them, we revere you with them, we invigorate you with them.

38,5. We address you as waters, fertile cows, mother-cows who are not to be killed for they nurse the poor and provide drink for all, you, the best and most beautiful ones, every time your long-armed munificence comes up to us, you good ones, you distributors, you pleasant ones, you mothers, you (sources of) gain.

Yasna 39

39,1 Herewith we worship the soul of the cow and (her) fashioner. (We worship) our own souls and the souls of the domestic animals, which seek refuge with us to whom they belong and with us who belong to them.

39,2. We worship the souls of the wild animals that are harmless. We worship the souls of the truthful men and women wherever they are born, whose better religious views prevail, will prevail, and have (always) prevailed.

39,3. Herewith we worship the good male and the good female (entities), who are holy and immortal, who have eternal life and provide eternal benefit, the male ones who dwell at the side of good thought, and the female ones who do so.

39,4. Just as you, O Ahura Mazdā, conceived, pronounced, created, and wrought all good (things), so we offer and commit (them) to you, so we worship you with them, so we revere you with them, so we invigorate you with them, O Mazdā Ahura.

39,5. We approach you with (our) relationship to a good family, to good truth, good joy, and good right-mindedness.

[1] In Avestan these are all of female gender, hence called 'women'.

Yasna 40

40,1. Āhū at̰ paitī adāhū mazdā ahurā mazdąmcā būiricā kərəšuuā rāitī tōi xrapaitī ahmat̰ hiiat̰ aibī. hiiat̰ mīždəm [m]auuaēϑəm[1] fradadāϑā daēnābiiō mazdā ahurā —

40,2. ahiiā huuō nə̄ dāidī ahmāicā ahuiiē manaxiiāicā tat̰ ahiiā yā tat̰ upā.jamiiāmā tauuacā haxəmā aṣ̌axiiācā vīspāi yauuē.

40,3. dāidī at̰ nərąš mazdā ahurā aṣ̌āunō aṣ̌acinaŋhō aidiiūš vāstriiəṇg darəgāi īžiiāi bəzuuaitē haxmainē ahmaibiiā.ahmā.rafənaŋhō.

40,4. aϑā xᵛaētūš aϑā vərəzə̄nā aϑā haxə̄mąm° xiiāt̰ yāiš hišcamaidē. aϑā və̄ utā xiiāmā mazdā ahurā ərəšiiā[2] ištəm rāitī.

Yasna 41

41,1. Stūtō garō vahmə̄ṇg ahurāi mazdāi aṣ̌āicā vahištāi dadəmahicā cīšmahicā ācā āuuaēdaiiamahī.

41,2. vohū xšaϑrəm tōi mazdā ahurā apaēmā vīspāi yauuē. huxšaϑrastū nə̄ nā vā nāirī vā xšaētā ubōiiō aŋhuuō hātąm hudāstəmā.

41,3. humāīm ϑβā īžīm yazatəm aṣ̌aŋhācim dadəmaidē. aϑā tū nə̄ gaiiascā astəṇtåscā xiiå ubōiiō aŋhuuō hātąm hudāstəmā.

41,4. hanaēmācā zaēmācā mazdā ahurā ϑβahmī rafənahī darəgāiiāu. aēšācā ə̄mauuaṇtascā buiiamā rapōišcā tū nə̄ darəgəmcā uštācā hātąm hudāstəmā.

41,5. ϑβōi staotarascā mąϑranascā ahurā mazdā aogəmadaēcā usmahicā vīsāmadaēcā. hiiat̰ mīždəm [m]auuaēϑəm fradadāϑā daēnābiiō mazdā ahurā —

41,6. ahiiā huuō nə̄ dāidī ahmāicā ahuiiē manaxiiāicā tat̰ ahiiā yā tat̰ upā.jamiiāmā tauuacā sarəm aṣ̌ahiiācā vīspāi yauuē.

End of Yasna Haptaŋhāiti[3]

---

[1] mīždəm mauuaēϑəm for mīždəm auuaēϑəm owing to erroneous segmentation of spoken text.
[2] ərəšiiā or ərəš́iiā?
[3] Yasna 42, the eighth chapter of the 'Yasna of Seven Chapters' (Yasna Haptaŋhāiti) is a later addition to this text.

Yasna 40

40,1. At these apportionments, O Mazdā Ahura, assume knowledge, and do it largely, of that which has form with us through your munificence. As to the firm prize which you (all) have presented to our religious views, O Mazdā Ahura:

40,2. Grant us (a share) of it for both this (material) existence and the spiritual[1] one, (grant us) that (share) of it through which we may come (and be in) your company and that of truth for all time.

40,3. Grant us, O Mazdā Ahura, truthful men who love truth, harmless herdsmen, for an everlasting, abundant, and permanent fellowship, offering support to us and enjoying support from us.

40,4. So may the families be, so the communities, and so the fellowships which we follow. So, O Mazdā Ahura, may we, the truthful, be in your favor on account of (our) appropriate offering of what is desired (by you).

Yasna 41

41,1. We offer, assign, and dedicate praises, songs, and glorifications to Mazdā Ahura and to best truth.

41,2. May we come (and be in) your good rule for all time, O Mazdā Ahura. May a good ruler, man or woman, assume rule over us in both existences, O most Munificent one among the existing.

41,3. We choose you, the blessed, abundant Yazata, who is in harmony with truth. So may you be for us both life and bodily frame in both existences, O most Munificent one among the existing!

41,4. May we deserve and win your long-time support, O Mazdā Ahura, and may we become vigorous and impetuous through you, and may you support us for a long time as (we) desire, O most Munificent one among the existing.

41,5. We declare ourselves your praisers and manthra-keepers, O Ahura Mazdā, and we are willing, and we are taking our positions (at the sacrifice). As to the firm prize which you (all) have presented to our religious views, O Mazdā Ahura:

41,6. Grant us (a share) of it for both this (material) existence and the spiritual one, that (share) of it through which we may come (and be in) your shelter and that of truth, for all time.

End of Yasna Haptanghāiti

[1] 'spiritual (existence), lit. 'mental (existence), (existence) of thought'.

Yasna 43-46. Uštauuaitī Gāϑā

Yasna 43. Uštauuaitī Hāiti

43,1. Uštā ahmāi yahmāi uštā kahmāicīṯ
vasə̄.xšaiiąs mazdā̊ dāiiāṯ ahurō
utaiiūitī təuuīšīm gaṯ.tōi[1] vasəmī
aṣ̌əm dərəidiiāi° taṯ mōi dā̊ ārmaitē
rāiiō aṣ̌īš vaŋhə̄uš gaēm manaŋhō

43,2. aṯcā ahmāi vīspanąm vahištəm
x^vāϑrōiiā nā x^vāϑrəm daidītā
ϑβā ciciϑβā° spə̄ništā mainiiū mazdā
yā̊[2] dā̊ aṣ̌ā vaŋhə̄uš māiiā̊ manaŋhō
vīspā aiiārə̄ darəgō.jiiātōiš° uruuādaŋhā

43,3. aṯ huuō vaŋhə̄uš vahiiō nā aibī.jamiiāṯ
yə̄ nā̊ ərəzūš sauuaŋhō paϑō sīšōiṯ
ahiiā aŋhə̄uš astuuatō manaŋhascā
haiϑiiə̄ṇg ā stīš[3] yə̄ṇg ā.šaēitī° ahurō
arədrō ϑβāuuąs huzə̄ṇtušə̄ spəṇtō mazdā

43,4. aṯ ϑβā mə̄ṇghāi taxməmcā spəṇtəm mazdā
hiiaṯ tā zastā yā tū haf̌šī auuā̊
yā̊ dā̊ aṣ̌īš drəguuāitē aṣ̌āunaēcā
ϑβahiiā garəmā āϑrō aṣ̌ā.aojaŋhō
hiiaṯ mōi vaŋhə̄uš hazə̄ jimaṯ manaŋhō

43,5. spəṇtəm aṯ ϑβā mazdā məṇ́hī° ahurā
hiiaṯ ϑβā aŋhə̄uš ząϑōi darəsəm paouruuīm
hiiaṯ dā̊ š́iiaoϑanā mīždauuąn yācā uxδā
akə̄m akāi vaŋ^vhīm° aṣ̌īm vaŋhaouuē
ϑβā hunarā dāmōiš uruuaēsē apə̄mē

43,6. yahmī spəṇtā ϑβā mainiiū uruuaēsē jasō
mazdā̊[4] xšaϑrā ahmī vohū manaŋhā
yehiiā š́iiaoϑanāiš gaēϑā̊ aṣ̌ā frādəṇtē
aēibiiō ratūš sə̄ṇghaitī ārmaitiš
ϑβahiiā xratə̄uš yə̄m naēciš dābaiieitī

[1] gaṯ.tōi, i.e. gatōi.
[2] yā̊, Geldner yā.
[3] ā stīš, Geldner astīš.
[4] mazdā̊ xšaϑrā, Geldner mazdā xšaϑrā.

Yasna 43 - 46. Ushtavaitī Gāthā

Yasna 43. Ushtavaitī Hāiti

43,1. I desire that stability and strength should come as desired, to whomsoever Mazdā Ahura, ruling as He desires, may grant what is desired.[1] O right-mindedness, grant me truth to keep it, (grant me) rewards of wealth and a life of good thought.

43,2. May the man obtain the best of all things, comfort in (the domain of) comfort,[2] (and) may he, perceptive through your most holy spirit, O Mazdā, (obtain) the blessings of good thought which you grant through truth, all (his) days along with the joy of long life.

43,3. May that man attain what is better than good, who could show us the straight paths of benefit of this material existence and that of thought, the true (paths) to the possessions where the Ahura dwells, the one such as you, zestful, bound (to us), and holy, O Mazdā.

43,4. I shall realize that you are firm and holy, O Mazdā, when the superiority of good thought comes to me from that hand with which you hold the rewards which you assign to the deceitful one and to the truthful one by the heat of your fire strong through truth.

43,5. I realize that you are holy, O Mazdā Ahura,[3] when I see you, the Primal one, at the procreation of existence (and) when you make actions reward-bearing as well as utterances, (assigning) evil to the evil one, but a good reward to the good one, by your skill, at the final turning point of the creation.[4] [5]

43,6. At the turning point to which you come with your holy spirit, being Mazdā through (your) power,[6] there through good thought by the actions of which the possessions are furthered through truth, right-mindedness pronounces judgments on these here, (the judgments) of your intellect, which nobody can deceive.

---

[1] 'desire ... desired ... desire ... desired', cf. 27,14, 46,12.

[2] 'in (the domain of) comfort', or: 'in search for comfort'?

[3] 'I recognize that you are holy, O Mazda Ahura': Zarathushtra is meditating in front of the sacrificial fire.

[4] 'final turning point of the creation' (hardly: 'final turning point of a creature') refers to the universal judgment rather than to the judgment at the end of one's individual life. Less clear 51,8.

[5] Zarathushtra is visualizing Ahura Mazda's activities both at the primal(?) creation and the final (?) judgment. The miraculousness of Ahura Mazda's power is described in a similar way in 31,7-8.

[6] 'being Mazdā through (your) power', i.e. 'being wise through (your) power'.

43,7 spəṇtəm at̰ ϑβā mazdā məŋ́hī° ahurā
hiiat̰ mā vohū pairī.jasat̰ manaŋhā
pərəsat̰cā mā ciš ahī kahiiā ahī
kaϑā aiiarə̄[1] daxšārā fərasaiiāi dīšā
aibī ϑβāhū gaēϑāhū tanušicā

43,8. at̰ hōi aojī zaraϑuštrō paouruuīm
haiϑiiō duuaēšā̊ hiiat̰ isōiiā drəguuāitē
at̰ aṣ̌āunē rafənō x́iiəm aojōŋhuuat̰°
hiiat̰ ā būštīš[2] vasasə.xšaϑrahiiā diiā
yauuat̰.ā[3] ϑβā mazdā staomī[4] ufiiācā

43,9. spəṇtəm at̰ ϑβā mazdā mə̄ŋ́hī° ahurā
hiiat̰ mā vohū pairī.jasat̰ manaŋhā
ahiiā fərasə̄m kahmāi vīuuīduiiē vašī
at̰ ā ϑβahmāi āϑrē rātąm nəmaŋhō
aṣ̌ahiiā mā yauuat̰ isāi maniiāi

43,10. at̰ tū mōi dāiš aṣ̌əm hiiat̰ mā zaozaomī
ārmaitī hacimnō īt̰ ārəm
pərəsācā nā̊ yā tōi ə̄hmā parštā
parštə̄m zī ϑβā yaϑənā[5] tat̰ ə̄mauuatąm
hiiat̰ ϑβā xšaiią̇s aēšəm diiāt̰ ə̄mauuaṇtəm

43,11. spəṇtəm at̰ ϑβā mazdā mə̄ŋ́hī° ahurā
hiiat̰ mā vohū pairī.jasat̰ manaŋhā
hiiat̰ xšmā uxδāiš dīdaiŋ́hē paouruuīm
sādrā mōi sąs maṣ̌iiaēšū zrazdāitiš°
tat̰ vərəziieidiiāi hiiat̰ mōi mraotā vahištəm

43,12. hiiat̰cā mōi mraoš aṣ̌əm jasō frāxšnənē
at̰ tū mōi nōit̰ asruštā pairiiaoγžā
uzirəidiiāi[6] parā hiiat̰ mōi ā.jimat̰
səraošō aṣ̌ī mązā.raiiā hacimnō
yā vī aṣ̌īš rānōibiiō sauuōi [vī]dāiiāt̰

43,13. spəṇtəm at̰ ϑβā mazdā mə̄ŋ́hī° ahurā
hiiat̰ mā vohū pairī.jasat̰ manaŋhā
arəϑā vōizdiiāi kāmahiiā tə̄m mōi dātā
darəgahiiā yaoš[7] yə̄m vā̊ naēciš° dārəšt itē
vairiiā̊ stōiš yā ϑβahmī xšaϑrōi vācī

[1] aiiarə, Geldner aiiārə.
[2] a būštīš, Geldner abūštīš.
[3] yauuat̰.a, i.e. yauuata.
[4] staomī, Geldner stāumī.
[5] yaϑənā, Geldner yaϑana.
[6] uzirəidiiāi, Geldner uzərədiiāi.
[7] yaoš, Geldner yāuš.

43,7. I realize that you are holy, O Mazdā Ahura, when one approaches me with good thought[1] and asks: "Who are you? To whom do you belong? Why do you wish a date for consultation, O zealous one, on your possessions and yourself?"

43,8. Then I say to him: "First, I am Zarathushtra. (Second), since I am a true person I seek to join enemies of the deceitful one. Thus I could be a strong support for the truthful one if I could gain the attributes of one who holds power at will as much as[2] I praise and extol you, O Mazdā."

43,9. I realize that you are holy, O Mazdā Ahura, when one approaches me with good thought. (Then) I ask:[3] "To whom do you want (me) to offer (a share) of this?"[4] To your fire, I will think the offering of reverence for truth for as long as I am able.

43,10. Thus show me the truth for which I am calling — I have come for it in agreement with right-mindedness — and ask us which are (the questions) to be asked you by us, for (a question) asked by you, is like (the question) of impetuous ones, (seeing) that a person who is in command of it could make you vigorous and impetuous.

43,11. I realize that you are holy, O Mazdā Ahura, when one approaches me with good thought. When, through utterances by you, I learn what is the first, (then) faith in mortals appears to me distressing. Let me do what you tell me to be the best.

43,12. And when you tell me, "with foresight you reach truth," then you give me orders not to be disobeyed. Let me arise before attention comes to me, followed by wealth-granting reward, which will distribute the rewards according to the balance at the (assignment of) benefit(s).

43,13. I realize that you are holy, O Mazdā Ahura, when one approaches me with good thought to take note of the aims of my wish. You have imparted that to me: (the wish) for a long life that nobody can oblige you to grant, and for a desirable possession which is said to be in your power.

---

[1] It is left open by Zarathushtra whether one should understand: 'when one approaches me with good thought', or: 'when one (such as you) approaches me with good thought'.

[2] 'as much as', more lit. 'through the intensity with which'.

[3] 'I ask': uncertain.

[4] '(a share) of this', i.e. a share of good thought?

43,14. hiiat̰ nā friiāi vaēdəmnō° isuuā dadīt̰
maibiiō mazdā tauuā rafənō fraxšnənəm
hiiat̰ ϑβā xšaϑrā ašāt̰ hacā fr̨aštā
uzirəidiiāi[1] azə̄[2] sarədanā̊ sə̄n̦ghahiiā
mat̰ tāiš vīspāiš yōi tōi mą̨ϑrā̊ marən̦tī

43,15. spən̦təm at̰ ϑβā mazdā mə̄ŋ́hī° ahurā
hiiat̰ mā vohū pairī.jasat̰ manaŋhā
daxšat̰ ušiiāi[3] tušnā maitiš vahištā
nōit̰ nā pourūš drəguuatō x́iiāt̰ cixšnušō
at̰ tōi vīspə̄n̦g an̦grə̄n̦g ašaonō[4] ādarə̄

43,16. at̰ ahurā huuō mainiiūm zaraϑuštrō
vərən̦tē mazdā yastē ciščā spə̄ništō
astuuat̰ ašəm x́iiāt̰ uštānā aojōŋhuuat̰°
xᵛə̄n̦g darəsōi xšaϑrōi x́iiāt̰ ārmaitiš
ašīm šiiaoϑanāiš vohū daidīt̰ manaŋhā

End of Yasna 43

---

[1] uzirəidiiāi, Geldner uzərədiiāi.
[2] azə, Geldner azəm.
[3] ušiiāi, or: ušiiai?
[4] ašaonō, Geldner ašāunō.

43,14. What a wealthy and powerful man would grant to a friend, (grant) me, O Mazdā, your support, and the foresight which you have obtained from truth, through your power, so that I may arise with all those who recite your manthras to drive away the challengers of (your) proclamation.

43,15. I realize that you are holy, O Mazdā Ahura, when one approaches me with good thought. Silent devotion suits best the intelligent one[1]. No man should seek to gratify the multitude of deceitful ones. These (deceitful ones), indeed, declare all harmful persons to be truthful.[2]

43,16. O Mazdā Ahura, this one, Zarathushtra,[3] chooses that very spirit which is your most holy one. May material truth strong through vitality be there in (full) view of the sun. May right-mindedness be in power. By actions may one give reward with good thought.

End of Yasna 43

[1] 'intelligent one': uncertain.
[2] The deceitful one declares the harmful (= deceitful) persons to be truthful, cf. 44,12.
[3] 'this one, Zarathushtra' is virtually as much as 'I, Zarathushtra'.

Yasna 44. Taṯ.ϑβā.pərəsā Hāiti

44,1. Taṯ ϑβā pərəsā ərəš mōi vaocā ahurā
nəmaŋhō ā yaϑā nəmə̄ xšmāuuatō
mazdā friiāi ϑβāuuąs saxiiāṯ mauuaitē
aṯ nə̄ aṣ̌ā friiā dazdiiāi hākurənā
yaϑā nə̄ ā vohū jimaṯ manaŋhā

44,2. taṯ ϑβā pərəsā ərəš mōi vaocā ahurā
kaϑā aŋhə̄uš vahištahiiā paouruuīm
kāϑə̄ sūidiiāi yə̄ ī paitišāṯ
huuō zī aṣ̌ā spəṇtō irixtəm vīspōibiiō
hārō mainiiū ahūm.biš° uruuaϑō mazdā

44,3. taṯ ϑβā pərəsā ərəš mōi vaocā ahurā
kasnā ząϑā ptā[1] aṣ̌ahiiā pouruiiō
kasnā xᵛə̄ṇg strə̄mcā[2] dāṯ aduuānəm
kə̄ yā mā̊ uxšiieitī nərəfsaitī ϑβaṯ
tācīṯ mazdā vasəmī aniiācā vīduiiē

44,4. taṯ ϑβā pərəsā ərəš mōi vaocā ahurā
kasnā dərətā ząmcā adə̄ nabā̊scā
auuapastōiš kə̄ apō uruuarā̊scā
kə̄ vātāi duuąnmaibiiascā yaogəṯ āsū
kasnā vaŋhə̄uš mazdā dąmiš manaŋhō

44,5. taṯ ϑβā pərəsā ərəš mōi vaocā ahurā
kə̄ huuāpā̊ raocā̊scā dāṯ təmā̊scā
kə̄ huuāpā̊ xᵛafnəmcā dāṯ zaēmācā
kə̄ yā ušā̊ arə̄m.piϑβā xšapācā
yā̊ manaoϑrīš cazdōŋhuuaṇtəm° arəϑahiiā

44,6. taṯ ϑβā pərəsā ərəš mōi vaocā ahurā
yā frauuaxšiiā yezī tā aϑā haiϑiiā
aṣ̌əm š́iiaoϑanāiš dəbązaitī ārmaitiš
taibiiō xšaϑrəm vohū cinas manaŋhā
kaēibiiō azīm rāniiō.skərəitīm° gąm tašō

44,7. taṯ ϑβā pərəsā ərəš mōi vaocā ahurā
kə̄ bərəxδąm tāšt xšaϑrā maṯ ārmaitīm
kə̄ uzəmə̄m cōrəṯ viiānaiiā puϑrəm piϑrē
azə̄m tāiš ϑβā fraxšnī auuāmī mazdā
spəṇtā mainiiū vīspanąm dātārəm

---

[1] ptā, Geldner patā.
[2] strə̄mcā, Geldner starə̄mcā.

Yasna 44. Tat-thwā-peresā Hāiti.

44,1. This I ask you, O Ahura, tell me truly: As for reverence — one such as you[1] should tell one such as me[2], your friend, how reverence to one such as you all[3] should be. Let friendly fellowships be granted to us by truth, so that one may come to us with good thought.

44,2. This I ask you, O Ahura, tell me truly: Of what kind is the first (stage) of best existence? The desired one who implements it so that we may enjoy benefit, that one indeed, holy through truth, watching with His spirit the outcome left for all, is the healer of existence, (our) ally, (you), O Mazdā.

44,3. This I ask you, O Ahura, tell me truly: Who, by procreation, is the primal father of truth? Who created the course of the sun and the stars? Through whom does the moon waxe and wane? These very things and others I wish to know, O Mazdā.

44,4. This I ask you, O Ahura, tell me truly: Who holds the earth down below? Who (prevents) the skies from falling? Who (preserves) the waters and the plants? Who yokes the swift teams to the wind and the clouds? Who is the creator of good thought, O Mazdā?

44,5. This I ask you, O Ahura, tell me truly: Which artisan created both light and darkness? Which artisan (created) both sleep and waking? Who is He through whom dawn, noon, and nightfall (succeed one another), which remind a conscientious person of his business?[4]

44,6. This I ask you, O Ahura, tell me truly, if what I am about to pronounce is really true: 'By (its) actions, right-mindedness consolidates truth, with good thought it commits the power to you"[5] — (if this is true then tell me): For whom did you fashion the joy-giving cow?

44,7. This I ask you, O Ahura, tell me truly: Who with His power fashioned esteemed right-mindedness? Who provides a father with a son outstanding in vitality? With these (questions) I prudently support you with holy spirit, you, the creator of all things, O Mazdā.

---

[1] 'one such as you' is as much as 'you' referring to Ahura Mazdā.
[2] 'one such as me' is as much as 'me' referring to Zarathushtra.
[3] 'one such as you all' is as much as 'you all' referring to the Ahuras.
[4] It is noteworthy that the prophet speaks of three ritual day-times only.
[5] The sentence 'By (its) actions ... power to you' is a manthra (truth spell) by which Zarathushtra tries to inspire Ahura Mazdā to answer the question 'for whom did you fashion the joy-giving cow?'

44,8. tat̰ ϑβā pərəsā ərəš mōi vaocā ahurā
mən̨dāidiiāi[1] yā tōi mazdā ādištiš
yācā vohū uxδā frašī manaŋhā
yācā aṣ̌ā aŋhə̄uš arəm vaēidiiāi°
kā mə̄ uruuā vohū uruuāxšat̰[2] āgəmat̰.tā

44,9. tat̰ ϑβā pərəsā ərəš mōi vaocā ahurā
kaϑā mōi yąm yaoš daēnąm [yaož]dānē°
yąm hudānaoš[3] paitišə saxiiāt̰ xšaϑrahiiā
ərəšuuā xšaϑrā ϑβāuuąs asīštiš° mazdā
hadəmōi aṣ̌ā vohucā šiiąs manaŋhā

44,10. tat̰ ϑβā pərəsā ərəš mōi vaocā ahurā
tąm daēnąm yā hātąm vahištā
yā mōi gaēϑå aṣ̌ā frādōit̰ hacə̄mnā
ārmatōiš uxδāiš šiiaoϑanā ərəš daidiiat̰
maxiiå cistōiš ϑβā ištiš° usə̄n mazdā

44,11. tat̰ ϑβā pərəsā ərəš mōi vaocā ahurā
kaϑā tə̄n̨g ā vījə̄miiāt̰ ārmaitiš
yaēibiiō mazdā ϑβōi vašiietē daēnā
azə̄m tōi āiš pouruiiō[4] frauuōiuuidē
vīspə̄n̨g aniiə̄n̨g mainiiə̄uš° spasiiā duuaēšaŋhā

44,12. tat̰ ϑβā pərəsā ərəš mōi vaocā ahurā
kə̄ aṣ̌auuā yāiš pərəsāi drəguuå vā
katārə̄m ā an̨grō vā huuō vā an̨grō
yə̄ mā drəguuå ϑβā sauuā paitī.ərətē
ciiə̄n̨ghat̰[5] huuō nōit̰ aiiə̄m an̨grō mainiietē°

44,13. tat̰ ϑβā pərəsā ərəš mōi vaocā ahurā
kaϑā drujəm nīš ahmat̰ [nīš.]nāšāmā
tə̄n̨g ā auuā yōi asruštōiš pərənåŋhō
nōit̰ aṣ̌ahiiā ādīuuiein̨tī hacə̄nā[6]
nōit̰ frasaiiā vaŋhə̄uš cāxnarə̄ manaŋhō

44,14. tat̰ ϑβā pərəsā ərəš mōi vaocā ahurā
kaϑā aṣ̌āi drujə̄m diiąm zastaiiō
nī hīm mərąždiiāi ϑβahiiā mąϑrāiš sə̄n̨ghahiiā
ə̄mauuaitīm sinąm dāuuōi drəguuasū
ā īš duuafšə̄n̨g mazdā [a]nāšē ąstąscā

---

[1] mən̨dāidiiāi, Geldner mən̨daidiiāi.
[2] uruuāxšat̰, Geldner uruuāšat̰.
[3] hudānaoš, Geldner hudānāuš.
[4] pouruiiō, var. pouruiiē.
[5] ciiə̄n̨ghat̰, reading doubtful, Geldner ciiaŋhat̰.
[6] hacə̄nā, Geldner hacə̄mnā.

44,8. This I ask you, O Ahura, tell me truly so that I may note in my mind, O Mazdā, your advice and (the words) on which I took counsel with both good thought and truth, with a view to a proper knowledge of existence. (Tell me:) Along which way will my soul meet the good things to come?

44,9. This I ask you, O Ahura, tell me truly: How may the Master of Power proclaim the religious view of a generous person, when I want to make it effective for myself, (how may He do so), one such as you, with (His) exalted power being in command of it, O Mazdā, dwelling in His place with truth and good thought?

44,10. This I ask you, O Ahura, tell me truly: Does the vigor of my insight (inspired) by you, O Mazdā, observe correctly and independently that religious view which is the best for those who exist[1] and which, in agreement with truth, may further my possessions through the action (inspired) by the utterances of right-mindedness?

44,11. This I ask you, O Ahura, tell me truly: How may right-mindedness spread to those to whom your religious view flows forth, O Mazdā? Together with these I am the first to commit myself to you. All others I look upon with hostility of my spirit.

44,12. This I ask you, O Ahura, tell me truly: Who is truthful? (Are these truthful) with whom I wish to take counsel, or the deceitful one?[2] Which of the two is it? Is the former harmful, or is the latter harmful, the deceitful one who (intends) to obstruct your benefactions?[3] Evidently, it is the latter and not the former who, being harmful, intends (to obstruct them).

44,13. This I ask you, O Ahura, tell me truly: How can we drive deceit out of ourselves (and) toward those who, stuffed with disobedience, neither strive for the benevolence of truth nor take pleasure in the consultation of good thought.

44,14. This I ask you, O Ahura, tell me truly: How can I deliver deceit into the hands of truth. Let one wipe it out with the manthras of your proclamation, let him place his forceful sword upon the deceitful ones to bring ill and harm over them, O Mazdā.

---

[1] 'the best for those who exist', lit. 'the best (among the views) of those who exist'.
[2] The deceitful one declares himself to be truthful, cf. 43,15.
[3] These are rhetorical questions.

44,15. tat̰ ϑβā pərəsā ərəš mōi vaocā ahurā
yezī ahiiā aṣ̌ā pōi mat̰ xšaiiehī
hiiat̰ hə̄m spādā anaocaŋhā jamaētē
auuāiš uruuātāiš yā tū mazdā dīdərəžō
kuϑrā aiiā̊ kahmāi vananąm dadā̊

44,16. tat̰ ϑβā pərəsā ərəš mōi vaocā ahurā
kə̄ vərəϑrəm.jā ϑβā pōi sə̄ṇghā yōi hə̄ṇtī
ciϑrā mōi dąm ahūm.biš° ratūm cīždī
at̰ hōi vohū sraošō jaṇtū manaŋhā
mazdā ahmāi yahmāi vašī kahmāicīt̰

44,17. tat̰ ϑβā pərəsā ərəš mōi vaocā ahurā
kaϑā mazdā zarəm carānī hacā xšmat̰
āskəitīm° xšmākąm hiiat̰cā mōi x́iiāt̰ vāxš aēšō
sarōi būždiiāi hauruuātā amərətātā
auuā mąϑrā yə̄ rāϑəmō aṣ̌āt̰ hacā

44,18. tat̰ ϑβā pərəsā ərəš mōi vaocā ahurā
kaϑā aṣ̌ā tat̰ mīždəm hanānī
dasā aspā̊ arš‹ə›nuuaitīš[1] uštrəmcā
hiiat̰ mōi mazdā apiuuaitī hauruuātā
amərətātā yaϑā hī taibiiō[2] dā̊ŋhā

44,19. tat̰ ϑβā pərəsā ərəš mōi vaocā ahurā
yastat̰ mīždəm hanəṇtē nōit̰ dāitī
yə̄ īt̰ ahmāi ərəžuxδā nā dāitē
kā tə̄m ahiiā maēniš[3] aŋhat̰ pouruiiē
vīduuā̊ auuąm yā īm aŋhat̰ apə̄mā

44,20. ciϑənā mazdā huxšaϑrā daēuuā ā̊ŋharə̄
at̰ īt̰ pərəsā yōi pišiieiṇtī aēibiiō kąm
yāiš gąm karapā usixšcā aēšəmāi dātā
yācā kauuā ąnmə̄nē[4] urūdōiiātā
nōit̰ hīm mīzə̄n[5] aṣ̌ā vāstrəm frādaiŋ́hē

End of Yasna 44

[1] arš‹ə›nuuaitīš, Geldner aršnauuaitīš.
[2] taibiiō, Geldner taēibiiō.
[3] maēniš, Geldner mainiš.
[4] ąnmə̄nē, var. ąnmə̄nī.
[5] hīm mīzə̄n, i.e. hīm [m]īzə̄n?

44,15. This I ask you, O Ahura, tell me truly, if (indeed) you have power to protect (me) with truth: When the two warring hosts confront each other, according to the rules which you wish to be enforced, to which of the two sides, to whom do you give victory, O Mazdā?

44,16. This I ask you, O Ahura, tell me truly: Who is a conquerer able to protect those who exist by your proclamation? As a judgment assign bright things to be in my house, O Healer of Existence. Let attention come to whomsoever you wish through good thought, O Mazdā.

44,17. This I ask you, O Ahura, tell me truly: How, with your agreement, can I reach my goal, your friendship, and that my voice be vigorous (enough) to win, for shelter, integrity and immortality through that manthra which depends on truth.

44,18. This I ask you, O Ahura, tell me truly: In truth, do I deserve that prize — ten mares with a stallion, and a camel — (a prize) which secures for me integrity and immortality, as you take them for yourself?[1]

44,19. This I ask you, O Ahura, tell me truly: If a person does not award such a prize to the man deserving it and hoping to get it due to a true utterance, then what punishment will befall that person in (his) first (existence)? (The punishment) that will befall him in the end (I myself) know.

44,20. O Mazdā, have there ever been Daēvas of good rule? But I ask that (of those) who deprive these (here) of their wish,[2] (obeying) those (words) with which the Karapan and the Usij take hold of the cow for wrathful treatment, as well as (those) with which the Kavi howls to the wind. They do not foster the (cow) whereby they could further the pasture through truth.

End of Yasna 44

[1] On the prize desired by Zarathushtra in order to enable him to propagate his religion, cf. 46,19.

[2] 'deprive ... of their wish': uncertain.

Yasna 45. At̰.frauuaxšiiā Hāiti

45,1. At̰ frauuaxšiiā nū gūšō.dūm° nū sraotā
yaēcā asnāt̰ yaēcā dūrāt̰ išaϑā
nū īm vīspā ciϑrə̄ zī mazdå̊ŋhō.dūm°
nōit̰ daibitīm duš.sastiš ahūm mərąšiiāt̰
akā varanā drəguuå̄ hizuuā[1] āuuarətō

45,2.at̰ frauuaxšiiā aŋhə̄uš mainiiū pouruiiē
yaiiå̄ spaniiå̄ ūitī mrauuat̰ yim aṇgrə̄m
nōit̰ nā manå̄ nōit̰ sə̄ṇghā nōit̰ xratauuō
naēdā varanā nōit̰ uxδā naēdā š́iiaoϑanā
nōit̰ daēnå̄ nōit̰ uruuąnō hacaiṇtē

45.3. at̰ frauuaxšiiā aŋhə̄uš ahiiā pouruuīm°
yąm[2] mōi vīduuå̄ mazdå̄ vaocat̰ ahurō
yōi īm və̄ noit̰ iϑā mąϑrəm varəšəṇtī
yaϑā īm mənāicā vaocacā
aēibiiō aŋhə̄uš auuōi aŋhat̰ apə̄məm

45,4. at̰ frauuaxšiiā aŋhə̄uš ahiiā vahištəm
aṣ̌āt̰ hacā mazdā vaēdā yə̄ īm dāt̰
ptarə̄m[3] vaŋhə̄uš varəzaiiaṇtō manaŋhō
at̰ hōi dugədā huš́iiaoϑanā ārmaitiš
nōit̰ diβžaidiiāi vīspā.hišas ahurō

45,5. at̰ frauuaxšiiā hiiat̰ mōi mraot̰ spəṇtō.təmō
vacə̄ srūidiiāi hiiat̰ marətaēibiiō vahištəm
yōi mōi ahmāi səraošəm dąn caiiascā
upā.jimən hauruuātā amərətātā
vaŋhə̄uš mainiiə̄uš° š́iiaoϑanāiš mazdå̄ ahurō

45,6. at̰ frauuaxšiiā vīspanąm mazištəm
stauuas aṣ̌ā yə̄ hudå̄ yōi hə̄ṇtī
spəṇtā mainiiū sraotū mazdå̄ ahurō
yehiiā vahmē vohū frašī manaŋhā
ahiiā xratū frō mā sāstū vahištā

45,7. yehiiā sauuā išå̄ṇtī rādaŋhō
yōi zī juuā å̄ŋharəcā buuaiṇticā
amərətāitī aṣ̌aonō[4] uruuā aēšō
utaiiūtā yā nərąš sādrā drəguuatō
tācā xšaϑrā mazdå̄ dąmiš ahurō

[1] hizuuā, Geldner hizuuå̄.
[2] yąm, Geldner ya, but see his Additions.
[3] ptarəm, Geldner patarəm. — [4]aṣ̌aonō, Geldner aṣ̌āunō.

Yasna 45. At-fravaxshyā Hāiti

45,1. Now I shall proclaim, listen now, hear now, O you, who are approaching from near and far, now take note of the world for it is bright. May the deceitful blasphemer,[1] by his evil choice, not destroy the (world) a second time with his tongue through preference being given to him.[2]

45,2. Now I shall proclaim the two spirits in the first (stage) of existence, of whom the holy one shall address the harmful one as follows: "Neither our thoughts nor pronouncements, neither intellects nor choices, neither utterances nor actions nor religious views, nor our souls are in agreement."

45,3. Now I shall proclaim the first of this existence, (the manthra) which Mazdā Ahura, the Knowing one, told me (saying): "For those among you who will not practice that manthra in the way I think and pronounce it, for them 'woe' will be the last word of (their) existence."

45,4. Now I shall proclaim the best of this existence. In accordance with truth I know Him, who created it, (I know Him), the father of abundant good thought, O Mazdā, and His daughter (is) right-mindedness of good works.[3] The all-seeing Ahura is undeceivable.

45,5. Now I shall proclaim the word which the most holy one pronounced to me, (and) which is best for mortals to listen to. Whoever shows me obedience to it will attain integrity and immortality. Through the actions of good spirit the Ahura (presents Himself) as Mazdā.

45,6. Now I shall proclaim the Greatest of All, praising with truth (Him) who is munificent to those who exist. Let Mazdā Ahura listen with holy spirit, let Him teach me the best (things) with His intellect, (Him) in whose glorification I take counsel with good thought.

45,7. (The truthful one) whose benefits the Bounteous ones implement[4] — those who exist[5], have existed, and will exist — the soul of the truthful one (will be) vigorous in immortality and in stability. The things which distress the deceitful men, also of these things Mazdā Ahura is the creator through (His) power.

---

[1] 'the deceitful blasphemer', i.e. Yima, cf. 32,8-9.
[2] 'by preference being given (to him)', or simply: 'by being invited', cf. 30,2, 45,8.
[3] 'His daughter, right-mindedness of good works': right-mindedness is the sister of good thought.
[4] 'whose benefits the Bounteous ones (i.e. the Ahuras) implement (or: set in motion)', or: 'whose benefits the Bounteous ones approach', or also: 'with whose benefit the Bounteous ones approach'?
[5] 'who exist', lit. 'who are alive'.

45,8. tə̄m nə̄ staotāiš nəmaŋhō ā.vīuuarəšō
nū zī̆t cašmainī viiādarəsəm
vaŋhə̄uš mainiiə̄uš° šiiaoϑanahiiā uxδaxiiācā
vīduš aṣ̌ā yim mazdąm ahurəm
at̰ hōi vahmə̄ṇg dəmānē garō nidāmā

45,9. tə̄m nə̄ vohū mat̰ manaŋhā cixšnušō
yə̄ nə̄ usə̄n cōrət̰ spə̄ṇcā aspə̄ṇcā
mazdā̊ xšaϑrā varəzī[1] nā̊° diiāt̰ ahurō
pasūš vīrə̄ṇg ahmākə̄ṇg fradaϑāi.ā
vaŋhə̄uš aṣ̌ā haoząϑβāt̰ ā manaŋhō

45,10. tə̄m nə̄ yasnāiš ārmatōiš mimaγžō
yə̄ ąnmə̄nī mazdā̊ srāuuī ahurō
hiiat̰ hōi aṣ̌ā vohucā cōišt manaŋhā
xšaϑrōi hōi hauruuātā amərətātā
ahmāi stōi dąn təuuīšī utaiiūitī

45,11. yastā daēuuə̄ṇg aparō maṣ̌iiąscā
tarə̄.mąstā yōi īm tarə̄.mainiiaṇtā°
aniiə̄ṇg ahmāt̰ yə̄ hōi arə̄m mainiiātā°
saošiiaṇtō də̄ṇg patōiš spəṇtā daēnā
uruuaϑō brātā[2] ptā[3] vā mazdā ahurā

End of Yasna 45

---

[1] varəzī nā̊, Geldner vərəzə̄niiā.
[2] brātā, Geldner barātā.
[3] ptā, Geldner patā.

45,8. Wishing to invite Him, Mazdā Ahura,[1] with the praises of our reverence, I have seen (Him) in my eye(s) just now, I, a truthful witness to the action and the utterance of the good spirit. For Him we lay down glorifications in the house of song..

45,9. Him I wish to gratify with our good thought, Him who at will produces for us fortune or misfortune. May the Ahura, Mazdā through His power,[2] place us in abundance in order to further our cattle and men in accordance with the bond of good thought with truth.

45,10. Him, the Ahura, who is heard as Mazdā[3] in (my) breath, Him I wish to present with the worships (inspired) by our right-mindedness. Let them place for Him integrity and immortality, strength and stability in the power that has been committed to Him through truth and good thought.

45,11. The other one[4] who therefore scorns the Daēvas and (evil) mortals who scorn Him, unlike the one who thinks about Him in the proper way, by the holy religious view of the beneficent lord of the house (he is cared for like) an ally, a brother, or (even his) father, O Mazdā Ahura.[5]

End of Yasna 45

[1] 'wishing to invite Him', or: 'giving preference to Him'?
[2] 'Mazdā through His power', i.e. 'wise through His power'.
[3] 'as Mazdā', i.e. 'as the Wise one'.
[4] 'the other one', i.e. Zarathushtra.
[5] The stanza is a compliment to Kavi Vishtāspa, the host of the prophet.

Yasna 46. Kamnamaēzā Hāiti

46,1. Kąm° nəmōi ząm   kuθrā nəmōi aiienī
pairī xᵛaētəuš   airiiamnascā° dadaitī
nōit̰ mā xšnāuš   yā vərəzənā həcā
naēdā daxiiəuš   yōi sāstārō drəguuaṇtō
kaθā θβā   xšnaošāi mazdā ahurā

46,2. vaēdā tat̰ yā   ahmī mazdā anaēšō
mā kamnafšuuā   hiiat̰cā kamnānā ahmī
gərəzōi tōi   ā īt̰ [a]uuaēnā ahurā
rafəδrəm caguuā̊   hiiat̰ friiō friiāi daidīt̰
āxsō vaŋhəuš   aṣ̌ā īštīm manaŋhō

46,3. kadā mazdā   yōi uxšānō asnąm
aŋhəuš darəθrāi   frō aṣ̌ahiiā [fr]ārəṇtē
vərəzdāiš sə̄ṇghāiš   saošiiaṇtąm xratauuō
kaēibiiō ūθāi   vohū jimat̰ manaŋhā
maibiiō θβā   sąstrāi vərənē ahurā

46,4. at̰ təṇg drəguuā̊   yə̄ṇg aṣ̌ahiiā važdrə̄ṇg pāt̰
gā̊ frōrətōiš   šōiθrahiiā vā daxiiəuš vā
dužazōbā̊ hąs   xᵛāiš š́iiaoθanāiš ahəmustō
yastəm xšaθrāt̰   mazdā mōiθat̰ jiiātəuš vā
huuō təṇg frō.gā̊   paθmə̄ṇg hucistōiš carat̰[1]

46,5. yə vā xšaiiąs   adąs drītā aiiaṇtəm
uruuātōiš vā   huzəṇtuš miθrōibiiō vā
rašnā juuąs   yə aṣ̌auuā drəguuaṇtəm
vīcīrō hąs   tat̰ frō xᵛaētauuē mruiiāt̰
uzūiθiiōi īm   mazdā xrūniiāt̰ ahurā

46,6. at̰ yastəm nōit̰   nā isəmnō āiiāt̰
drūjō huuō   dāmąn haēθahiiā[2] gāt̰
huuō zī drəguuā̊   yə drəguuāitē vahištō
huuō aṣ̌auuā   yahmāi aṣ̌auuā friiō
hiiat̰ daēnā̊   paouruiiā̊ dā̊ ahurā

46,7. kə̄mnā° mazdā   mauuaitē pāiiūm dadā̊[3]
hiiat̰ mā drəguuā̊   dīdarəšata aēnaŋ́hē°
aniiəm θβahmāt̰   āθrascā manaŋhascā
yaiiā̊ š́iiaoθanāiš   aṣ̌əm θraoštā ahurā
tąm mōi dąstuuąm   daēnaiiāi frauuaocā

---

[1] carat̰, Geldner carāt̰.
[2] haēθahiia, Geldner haiθiia.
[3] dadā̊, Geldner dadāt̰.

Yasna 46. Kamnamaēzā Hāiti

46,1. Where and which part of land shall I go to succeed?[1] They keep me away from the family and the tribe. The community[2] that I wish to join does not gratify me, nor do the deceitful tyrants of the land. How shall I gratify you, O Mazdā Ahura?

46,2. I know why I am lacking in vigor. It is because of the scantiness of my livestock and because I only have few men.[3] I complain to you, look hither, O Mazdā Ahura. Extend (to me) such support as a friend would grant to a friend. Look at the vigor of good thought (inspired) by truth.

46,3. When will the bulls of the days, the intellects of the benefactors,[4] rise above the world with increased proclamations (for people) to grasp truth? To which people will one come with good thought to provide them with nourishment? I choose you, O Mazdā Ahura, to tell me (that).

46,4. Yet the deceitful one, having evil spells and being discontent with his own actions, prevents those bulls which pull the wagon of truth,[5] from rising above county and land.[6] The person who deprives him of his power and livelihood, O Mazdā, will render those bulls the leaders[7] of the flight of the good insight.

46,5. If a truthful person, living lawfully and holding power with judicial authority, wishes to accomodate and (thereby) keep a deceitful person who comes to him, being bound (to him) by virtue of stipulation or contract, then (that truthful person) should inform his family in order to protect him against bloodshed, O Mazdā Ahura.[8]

46,6. But if (a deceitful person) should come to him with no claim, then for partnership let that man go to the abodes of deceit. That person is deceitful who is best to the deceitful one,[9] and that person is truthful to whom the truthful one is a friend. (This is) how you established the primal religious views, O Ahura.

46,7. O Mazdā, whom do you appoint as a guardian for one such as me when a deceitful person tries to seize and injure me? Whom other (do you appoint) than your fire and your thought, by whose actions truth is nourished? Proclaim this information for my religious view.

---

[1] Uncertain. More literally perhaps: 'To which piece of land (shall I go) to (find) pasture? Where shall I go to (find) pasture?

[2] 'family ... tribe ... community' is an elaboration of the series 'family - community - tribe'.

[3] 'I only have few men' refers to the small number of the prophet's adherents and attendants.

[4] 'the bulls of the days, the intellects of the benefactors': Introd. 5.3.

[5] 'which pull the wagon of truth', lit. 'the draught-animals of truth'.

[6] 'county and land' is abbreviated from the standard series 'house - village - county - land'.

[7] 'will render those bulls the leaders of the flight', lit. 'will render them leading bulls of the flight'.

[8] The stanza offers typical examples of appositional word-order.

[9] 'best to the deceitful one', i.e. 'familiar with the deceitful one', cf. 33,3,

46,8. yə̄ vā mōi yā̊ gaēϑā̊ dazdē aēnaŋ́hē°
nōiṯ ahiiā mā āϑriš šiiaoϑanāiš frōsiiāṯ
paitiiaogəṯ tā ahmāi jasōiṯ duuaēšaŋhā
tanuuə̄m ā yā īm hujiiātōiš pāiiāṯ
nōiṯ dužjiiātōiš kācīṯ mazdā duuaēšaŋhā

46,9. kə̄ huuō yə̄ mā arədrō cōiϑaṯ pouruiiō
yaϑā ϑβā zəuuīštīm uzə̄mōhī°
šiiaoϑanōi spəṇtəm ahurəm aṣ̌auuanəm
yā tōi aṣ̌ā yā aṣ̌āi gə̄uš tašā mraoṯ
išəṇtī mā tā tōi vohū manaŋhā

46,10. yə̄ vā mōi nā gənā vā mazdā ahurā
dāiiāṯ aŋhə̄uš yā tū vōistā vahištā
aṣ̌īm aṣ̌āi vohū xšaϑrəm manaŋhā
yąscā haxšāi xšmāuuatąm vahmāi.ā
frō tāiš vīspāiš cinuuatō [fra]frā pərətūm

46,11. xšaϑrāiš yūjə̄n karapanō kāuuaiiascā
akāiš šiiaoϑanāiš ahūm mərəṇgəidiiāi maṣ̌īm
yə̄ṇg xᵛə̄ uruuā xᵛaēcā xraodaṯ daēnā
hiiaṯ aibī.gəmən yaϑrā cinuuatō pərətuš
yauuōi vīspāi drūjō dəmānāi astaiiō

46,12. hiiaṯ us aṣ̌ā naptiiaēšū nafšucā
tūrahiiā [uz]jə̄n friiānahiiā aojiiaēšū
ārmatōiš gaēϑā̊ frādō ϑβaxšaŋhā
aṯ īš vohū hə̄m.aibī.mōist manaŋhā
aēibiiō rafəδrāi mazdā̊ sastē ahurō

46,13. yə̄ spitāməm zaraϑuštrəm rādaŋhā
marətaēšū xšnāuš huuō nā frasrūidiiāi° ərəϑβō[1]
aṯ hōi mazdā̊ ahūm dadāṯ ahurō
ahmāi gaēϑā̊ vohū frādaṯ manaŋhā
tə̄m və̄ aṣ̌ā mə̄hmaidī huš.haxāim

46,14. zaraϑuštrā kastē aṣ̌auuā uruuaϑō
mazōi magāi kə̄ vā frasrūidiiāi° vaštī
aṯ huuō kauuā vīštāspō yāhī
yə̄ṇgstū mazdā hadəmōi minaš ahurā
tə̄ṇg zbaiiā vaŋhə̄uš uxδāiš manaŋhō

46,15. haēcaṯ.aspā vaxšiiā və̄ spitamā̊ŋhō
hiiaṯ dāϑə̄ṇg vīcaiiaϑā adāϑąscā
tāiš yūš šiiaoϑanāiš aṣ̌əm xšmaibiiā daduiiē
yāiš dātāiš paouruiiāiš ahurahiiā
{ *one line of the stanza is missing* }

---

[1] ərəϑβō, Geldner ərəδβō.

46,8. And if someone should plan to destroy my possessions, then may destruction not reach me through his actions. May these (actions) fall back upon him with hostility, onto his body, and prevent him from having a good life, not (prevent him) from having a bad life. Each of them with hostility, O Mazdā.

46,9. Who is the zestful one who would be be the first to learn from me how I have valued you, the truthful Ahura, as being most swift and holy in action? The (words) that the fashioner of the cow speaks to you, with truth, (and) to truth,[1] about that one who could invigorate me,[2] those (words he speaks) to you with good thought.

46,10. O Mazdā Ahura, whosoever, man or woman, gives me those things which you know are the best of existence: reward for truth and power through good thought, and whom I stimulate to glorify those such as you, with all those I will cross over the Account-keeper's Bridge.

46,11. Through their power the Karapans and the Kavis yoke the mortal one to evil actions in order to destroy existence. When they reach the Account-keeper's Bridge their own soul(s) and their own religious view(s) will make them tremble, and they will be guests in the house of deceit for all time.

46,12. When Mazdā Ahura with truth rises among the reputable relatives and descendants of Tūra, son of Friya who furthered the possessions of right-mindedness with zeal, then He joins them together with good thought to command them for (their) support.

46,13. That man among mortals is worthy of being celebrated who has gratified Spitama Zarathushtra with bounteousness. Mazdā Ahura grants him existence, and He furthers his possessions through good thought. We recognize him to be a good friend of your truth.

46,14. O Zarathushtra, who is your truthful ally for the great offering? Who wishes to be celebrated? Here Kavi Vishtaspa (wishes to be celebrated) at the sharing. Those whom you are fostering in their place, those I will invoke with the utterances of good thought.

46,15. O members of the Haēchataspa Spitama family, I shall tell you now that you shall discriminate between the just and the unjust. You will obtain truth through those actions which (follow) the primal laws of the Ahura — {*one line of the stanza is missing*}.

[1] 'to you, with truth, (and) to truth': uncertain.
[2] 'who could invigorate me', or: 'who would approach me'? The entire passage is enigmatic.

46,16. fərašaoštrā aϑrā tū arədrāiš idī
huuō.guuā tāiš yə̄ṇg usuuahī uštā stōi
yaϑrā aṣ̌ā hacaitē ārmaitiš
yaϑrā vaŋhə̄uš manaŋhō īštā xšaϑrəm
yaϑrā mazdā̊ varədəmąm šaēitī ahurō

46,17. yaϑrā və̄ afšmānī sə̄ṇghānī
nōit̰ anafšmąm də̄jāmāspā huuō.guuā
hadā və̄stā vahmə̄ṇg səraošā rādaŋhō
yə̄ vīcinaot̰ dāϑəmcā adāϑəmcā
daŋrā° maṇtū aṣ̌ā mazdā̊ ahurō

46,18. yə̄ maibiiā yaoš ahmāi ‹h›ascīt̰ vahištā
maxiiā̊ ištōiš vohū cōišəm manaŋhā
ąstə̄ṇg ahmāi yə̄ nā̊ ąstāi daidītā
mazdā aṣ̌ā xšmākəm vārəm xšnaošəmnō
tat̰ mōi xratə̄uš manaŋhascā vīciϑəm

46,19. yə̄ mōi aṣ̌āt̰ haiϑīm hacā varəšaitī
zaraϑuštrāi hiiat̰ vasnā fərašō.təməm
ahmāi mīždəm hanəṇtē parāhūm
manə̄.vistāiš mat̰ vīspāiš gāuuā azī
tācīt̰ mōi sąs tuuə̄m mazdā vaēdištō

End of Yasna 46

46,16. O Frashaoshtra Hvōguva, come with the zestful ones whom we desire to be as they desire,[1] to the place where right-mindedness is in agreement with truth, where power is in command of good thought, and where Mazdā Ahura dwells in prosperity.

46,17. (Come to the place) where I shall proclaim for you (in) verses, and not (in) non-verses, O Jāmāspa Hvōguva, (proclaim) glorifications for you in obedience to bountiful Mazdā Ahura, who discriminates between the just one and the unjust one with His prudent counselor, truth.

46,18. The person who is pure-in-heart toward me, I for my part assign to him the best things in my command, through good thought, but harm to him who schemes to harm us, O Mazdā, thereby gratifying your will by truth. Such is the discrimination made by my intellect and thought.

46,19. The person who, through truth, makes real for me that which is most brilliant in value, for Zarathushtra, who deserves a prize providing higher life — two fertile cows along with all imaginable things — through that very person you, O Mazdā, reveal yourself to me as the best provider.[2]

End of Yasna 46

[1] 'desire ... desire', cf. 27,14, 43,1.
[2] As to the prize cf. 44,18.

Yasna 47-50. Spəṇtā.mainiiu Gāϑā

Yasna 47. Spəṇtā.mainiiu Hāiti

47,1. Spəṇtā mainiiū vahištācā manaŋhā
hacā ašāṯ šiiaoϑanācā vacaŋhācā
ahmāi dąn hauruuātā amərətātā
mazdå xšaϑrā ārmaitī ahurō

47,2. ahiiā mainiiəuš° spəništahiiā vahištəm
hizuuā uxδāiš vaŋhəuš əəānū manaŋhō
ārmatōiš zastōibiiā šiiaoϑanā vərəziiaṯ
ōiiā cistī huuō pta[1] ašahiiā mazdå

47,3. ahiiā mainiiəuš° tuuəm ahī ‹p›tā[2] spəṇtō
yə̄ ahmāi gąm rāniiō.skərəitīm° hə̄m.tašaṯ
aṯ hōi vāstrāi rāmā.då ārmaitīm
hiiaṯ hə̄m vohū mazdā [hə̄mə.]fraštā manaŋhā

47,4. ahmāṯ mainiiəuš° rārəšiieiṇtī drəguuaṇtō
mazdā spəṇtāṯ nōiṯ iϑā ašaonō[3]
kasəušcīṯ nā ašāunē kāϑē aŋhaṯ
isuuācīṯ hąs paraoš akō drəguuāitē

47,5. tācā spəṇtā mainiiū mazdā ahurā
ašāunē cōiš yā zī cīcā vahištā
hanarə ϑβahmāṯ zaošāṯ drəguuå baxšaitī
ahiiā šiiaoϑanāiš akāṯ ā šiiąs[4] manaŋhō

47,6. tā då spəṇtā mainiiū mazdā ahurā
āϑrā vaŋhāu vīdāitīm rānōibiiā
ārmatōiš dəbązaŋhā ašaxiiācā
hā zī pourūš išəṇtō vāurāitē

End of Yasna 47

---

[1] pta, Geldner patā.
[2] tā spəṇtō for ptā spəṇtō by dissimilation in the oral tradition.
[3] ašaonō, Geldner ašāunō.
[4] ā šiiąs, Geldner ašiiąs.

Yasna 47-50. Spentāmainyu Gāthā

Yasna 47. Spentāmainyu Hāiti

47,1. With holy spirit and best thought, with action and word in accordance with truth, they shall offer Him integrity and immortality.[1] The Ahura is Mazdā[2] through (His) power (and) right-mindedness.

47,2. The best (manifestation) of this most holy spirit: the actions of right-mindedness (performed) with hands and (inspired) by the utterances (spoken) by tongue in pursuit of good thought, (these) one performs with this realization: "He, Mazdā, is the father of truth."[3]

47,3. You are the holy father of this spirit who fashioned for it the joy-giving cow, and in order to establish peace for her pasture (fashioned) right-mindedness when He took counsel with good thought.

47,4. The deceitful rip away from this holy spirit those who are not really truthful, O Mazdā. A man of even little (means) shall behave kindly to the truthful one, and even an owner of much (wealth shall be) evil to the deceitful one.

47,5. And through this holy spirit, O Mazdā Ahura, you assign to the truthful one whatever best things the deceitful one, removed from your approval, must give up, dwelling at the side of evil thought on account of his actions.

47,6. Through this holy spirit, O Mazdā Ahura, you have established the distribution (to be performed) in the good (way)[4] with fire, according to the balance, on account of the solidity of right-mindedness and truth. This (distribution) indeed shall win over the many who approach.

End of Yasna 47

[1] 'offer Him integrity and immortality': Introd. 5.1.
[2] 'the Ahura is Mazdā', i.e. 'the Ahura is wise'.
[3] 'He, Mazdā, is the father of truth', or: 'He is the wise father of truth.'
[4] 'in the good (way)', or: 'at the good (reward to be distributed)'.

Yasna 48. Yeziδā Hāiti

48,1. yezī adāiš aṣ̌ā drujəm vāṇghaitī[1]
hiiat̰ ąsašutā[2] yā daibitānā fraoxtā
amərətāitī daēuuāišcā maṣ̌iiāišcā
at̰ tōi sauuāiš vahməm vaxšat̰ ahurā

48,2. vaocā mōi yā tuuə̄m vīduuå ahurā
parā hiiat̰ mā yā məṇg pərəϑā jimaitī
kat̰ aṣ̌auuā mazdā vāṇghat̰ drəguuaṇtəm
hā zī aŋhə̄uš vaŋᵛhī° vistā ākərəitiš°

48,3. at̰ vaēdəmnāi vahištā sāsnanąm
yąm hudå sāstī aṣ̌ā ahurō
spəṇtō vīduuå yaēcīt̰ gūzrā sə̄ṇghåŋhō
ϑβāuuąs mazdā vaŋhə̄uš xraϑβā manaŋhō

48,4. yə̄ dāt̰ manō vahiiō mazdā aš́iiascā
huuō daēnąm š́iiaoϑanācā vacaŋhācā
ahiiā zaošə̄ṇg uštiš varənə̄ṇg hacaitē
ϑβahmī xratāu[3] apə̄məm nanā aŋhat̰

48,5. huxšaϑrā xšə̄ṇtąm mā nə̄ dušəxšaϑrā° xšə̄ṇtā
vaŋhuiiå cistōiš š́iiaoϑanāiš ārmaitē
yaoždå maṣ̌iiāi aipī ząϑəm vahištā
gauuōi vərəziiātąm tąm nə̄ xᵛarəϑāi fšuiiō

48,6. hā zī nə̄ hušōiϑəmā hā nə̄ utaiiūitīm
dāt̰ təuuīšīm vaŋhə̄uš manaŋhō bərəxδē
at̰ axiiāi aṣ̌ā mazdå uruuarå vaxšat̰
ahurō aŋhə̄uš ząϑōi paouruiiehiiā

48,7. nī aēšəmō [nī.]diiātąm paitī rəməm [paitī.]siiōdūm[4]
yōi ā vaŋhə̄uš manaŋhō dīdraγžō.duiiē°
aṣ̌ā viiąm yehiiā hiϑāuš nā spəṇtō
at̰ hōi dāmąm ϑβahmī ā dąm ahurā

48,8. kā tōi vaŋhə̄uš mazdā xšaϑrahiiā īštiš
kā tōi aṣ̌ōiš ϑβahiiå maibiiō ahurā
kā ϑβōi aṣ̌ā ākå arədrə̄ṇg išiiā
vaŋhə̄uš mainiiə̄uš° š́iiaoϑananąm jauuarō

---

1 vəṇghaitī, Geldner vəṇŋhaitī.
2 ąsašutā, lapsus for ąsaš.tā (i.e ąsaš tā or ąsaštā), or slightly incorrect for ąsa-šūtā, or blunder for ąsaēšū tā?
3 xratāu, Geldner xratå.
4 siiōdūm, Geldner siiōzdūm.

Yasna 48. Yezidhā Haiti

48,1. If truths[1] can defeat deceit through these (activities)[2] so that those (lies) about immortality which have been proclaimed again and again by Daēvas and (evil) mortals will receive (their) due share,[3] then one will increase your glorification on account of (your) benefactions, O Ahura.

48,2. Tell me, O Mazdā Ahura, what you know, (already) before the penalties (imposed on the deceitful) which I have in mind can reach me. Will the truthful one defeat the deceitful one? For such a shaping of existence has been found to be good.

48,3. The best of teachings is for him who has (already) taken possession (of it in his thought), (the teaching) that the munificent holy Ahura, who knows even the secret proclamations, teaches with truth and with the intellect of good thought, one such as you, O Mazdā.

48,4. He who manifests now better, now worse thought, O Mazdā, he (manifests his) religious view. By action and word he follows his pleasures, desires, and preferences. In the end he will be variously (recorded) in your intellect, here and there.

48,5. Let good rulers assume rule (over us), with actions of good insight, O right-mindedness. Let not bad rulers assume rule over us. The best (insight), which purifies progeny for mankind, let it also be applied to the cow. Her you breed for us for food.

48,6. Indeed, she gives us good dwelling, stability, and strength, O (right-mindedness) esteemed by good thought, and so Mazdā Ahura shall make the plants grow for her with truth, at the procreation of the first existence.

48,7. Let wrath be laid low. Strike your axe at fury, you who wish to attach yourselves to good thought. Let him whose partner is the holy man be protected by truth. His abodes are in your house, O Ahura.

48,8. What is the command of your good power, O Mazdā Ahura? What is (the command) of your reward for me? What is your (command) through truth, vigorosly facing the zestful ones, and serving as encouragement[4] for actions of good spirit.

---

[1] The plural of 'truth' is also found in 34,9.
[2] 'through these (activities)', or: 'through those (present)'?
[3] 'receive (their) due share': uncertain.
[4] 'encouragement': uncertain.

48,9. kadā vaēdā yezī cahiiā xšaiiaθā
mazdā aṣ̌ā yehiiā mā āiθiš duuaēθā
ərəš mōi [ərəž]ūcąm vaŋhəuš vafuš manaŋhō
vīdiiāt̰ saošiiąs yaθā hōi aṣ̌iš aŋhat̰

48,10. kadā mazdā mąnarōiš narō vīsəṇtē
kadā ajən mūθrəm ahiiā madahiiā[1]
yā aṇgraiiā karapanō urūpaiieiṇtī
yācā xratū dušəxšaθrā° dax́iiunąm

48,11. kadā mazdā aṣ̌ā mat̰ ārmaitiš
jimat̰ xšaθrā hušəitiš vāstrauuaitī
kōi drəguuō.dəbīš° xrūrāiš rāmąm dåṇtē
kəṇg ā vaŋhəuš jimat̰ manaŋhō cistiš

48,12. at̰ tōi aŋhən saošiiaṇtō dax́iiunąm
yōi xšnəm[2] vohū manaŋhā hacåṇtē
š́iiaoθanāiš aṣ̌ā θβahiiā mazdā səṇghahiiā
tōi zī dātā hamaēstārō aēšəm.mahiiā[3]

End of Yasna 48

[1] madahiiā, Geldner magahiiā.
[2] xšnəm, Geldner xšnūm.
[3] aēšəm.mahiiā, i.e. aēšəmahiiā.

48,9. When shall I know, O Mazdā, whether through truth you have control over anything, the fear of which frightens me. Let the pronouncement of good thought be told me truly. May the benefactor know of what kind his reward will be.

48,10. When, O Mazdā, will the men of the believer take (their) positions (at the sacrifice)? When will they kick over this urine-like intoxicant[1] with which the Karapans and the bad rulers of the lands (inspired) by their (bad) intellect, cause racking pain?

48,11. When, O Mazdā, will right-mindedness come with truth, through power provided with good dwelling and pasture? Who will establish peace with the bloodstained deceitful? To whom will the insight of good thought come?

48,12. Those will be the benefactors of lands who with good thought join in your recognition, with actions (inspired) by the truth of your proclamation, O Mazdā. For these (benefactors) are appointed to be removers of wrath.

End of Yasna 48

[1] 'this urine-like intoxicant': the Haoma Dūraosha, cf. 32,14.

Yasna 49. At̰.māiiauuā Hāiti

49,1. At̰ mā yauuā bə̄ṇduuō pafrē mazištō
yə̄ dušərəϑrīš cixšnušā aṣ̌ā mazdā
vaŋᵛhī° ādā gaidī mōi ā mōi [a]rapā
ahiiā vohū aošō vīdā manaŋhā

49,2. at̰ ahiiā mā bə̄ṇduuahiiā mānaiieitī
t̰kaēšō drəguuā̊ daibitā aṣ̌āt̰ rārə̄šō
nōit̰ spəṇtąm dōrəšt ahmāi stōi ārmaitīm
naēdā vohū mazdā fraštā manaŋhā

49,3. at̰cā ahmāi varənāi mazdā nidātəm
aṣ̌əm sūidiiāi t̰kaēšāi rāšaiieŋ́hē druxš
tā vaŋhə̄uš sarə̄ iziiā[1] manaŋhō
antarə̄ vīspə̄ṇg drəguuatō haxmə̄ṇg [antarə̄.]mruiiē

49,4. yōi duš.xraϑβā aēšəməm varədən rāməmcā
xᵛāiš hizubīš fšuiiasū afšuiiaṇtō
yaēšąm nōit̰ huuaršštāiš vąs dužuuaršštā
tōi daēuuə̄ṇg dąn yā drəguuatō daēnā

49,5. at̰ huuō mazdā īžācā āzūitišcā
yə̄ daēnąm vohū sārəštā° manaŋhā
ārmatōiš kascīt̰ aṣ̌ā huzə̄ṇtuš
tāišcā vīspāiš ϑβahmī xšaϑrōi ahurā

49,6. frō vā̊ [fra]ēšiiā mazdā aṣ̌əmcā mrūitē
yā və̄ xratə̄uš xšmākahiiā ā.manaŋhā[2]
ərəš vīcidiiāi yaϑā ī srāuuaiiaēmā
tąm daēnąm yā xšmāuuatō ahurā

49,7. tat̰cā vohū mazdā sraotū manaŋhā
sraotū aṣ̌ā gūšahuuā tū ahurā
kə̄ airiiamā kə̄ xᵛaētuš dātāiš aŋhat̰
yə̄ vərəzə̄nāi vaŋᵛhīm° dāt̰ frasastīm

49,8. fərašaoštrāi uruuāzištąm aṣ̌ahiiā dā̊
sarə̄m tat̰ ϑβā mazdā yāsā ahurā
maibiiācā yąm vaŋhāu ϑβahmī ā xšaϑrōi
yauuōi vīspāi fraēštā̊ŋhō ā̊ŋhāmā

---

[1] iziiā, Geldner iziiāi.
[2] ā.manaŋhā, or: a manaŋhā?

Yasna 49. At-mā-yavā Hāiti

49,1. The 'great chief' Bendva has stuffed himself with barley.[1] O Mazdā, (come to me) who try to gratify the ill-warded (cows) with truth. Come to me as good apportionment, and support me. See to his elimination with good thought.

49,2. Similar to Bendva is his deceitful teacher[2] who again and again rips (people) away from truth. Neither does he grasp holy right-mindedness to be his, nor does he take counsel with good thought, O Mazdā.

49,3. And truth, O Mazdā, has been implanted in this (our) choice to benefit (us), but deceit (has been implanted) in (false) teaching in order to harm (people). Therefore I request the shelter of good thought, and I banish all the deceitful from (our) fellowship.

49,4. Those who (influenced) by the person of bad intellect increase wrath and fury with their tongues, being no cattle-breeders among the cattle-breeders, (people) whose bad deeds weigh down (the scale) because of their lacking in good deeds, such people establish the Daēvas[3], which is (in accordance with) the religious view of the deceitful one.

49,5. But that man is (personified) abundance and nourishment, who associates[4] his religious view with good thought and who by virtue of right-mindedness is bound to truth and to all those in your power, O Mazdā Ahura.

49,6. I urge you, O Mazdā Ahura, and truth, to tell me which are the passions of your intellect, so that we may discern truly how we could make known that religious view which is that of one such as you.

49,7. Let one hear this with good thought. Let one hear (it) with truth. Listen, O Mazdā Ahura. Which tribe, which family will be (there), who by (following your) laws will give the community a good reputation?[5]

49,8. Grant to Frashaoshtra and me the most delightful shelter of truth, which is in your good power. This I entreat you for, O Mazdā Ahura. Let us (all) be dearest friends[6] for all time.

---

[1] 'has stuffed himself with barley', or: 'has stuffed himself with my barley', or: 'has filled himself with beer', or: 'with (long)evity'?

[2] 'similar to Bendva is his deceitful teacher', or: '(in the entourage) of this Bendva there abides a deceitful teacher', or also: 'the deceitful teacher of this Bendva angers me'?

[3] 'establish the Daēvas', or: 'produce Daēvas'.

[4] 'associates', or: 'shelters'.

[5] 'tribe ... family ... to the community' is an elaboration of the series 'family - community - tribe'.

[6] 'dearest friends', or: 'messengers', but whose messengers?

49,9. sraotū sāsnå fšəŋ́hiiō° suiiē taštō
nōit̰ ərəš.vacå sarə̄m didąs drəguuātā
hiiat̰ daēnå vahištē yūjə̄n mīždē
aṣ̌ā yuxtā yāhī də̄jāmāspō

49,10. tat̰cā mazdā ϑβahmī ā dąm[1] nipåŋ́hē
manō vohū urunascā aṣ̌āunąm
nəmascā yā ārmaitiš īžācā
mązā.xšaϑrā vazdaŋhā auuə̄.mīrā[2]

49,11. at̰ dušəxšaϑrə̄ṇg duš.š́iiaoϑanə̄ṇg dužuuacaŋhō
duždaēnə̄ṇg dužmanaŋhō° drəguuatō
akāiš xᵛarəϑāiš paitī uruuąnō [paiti]ieiṇtī
drūjō dəmānē haiϑiiā aŋhən astaiiō

49,12. kat̰ tōi aṣ̌ā zbaiieṇtē auuaŋhō
zaraϑuštrāi kat̰ tōi vohū manaŋhā
yə̄ və̄ staotāiš mazdā frīnāi ahurā
auuat̰ yāsąs hiiat̰ və̄ ištā vahištəm

End of Yasna 49

---

[1] ā dąm, Geldner ādąm.
[2] auuə̄.mīrā, or: auuə̄m īrā? Geldner auuə̄mīrā.

49,9. Let the bondsman fashioned for benefit hear the teachings. The person of true speech does not approve of associating with the deceitful one. For the truthful yoke their religious views to the best prize, (being themselves) yoked to truth, at the sharing, O Jāmāspa.

49,10. In your house, O Mazdā, you store for yourself (our) good thought, the souls of the truthful, and the reverence with which right-mindedness (is associated), as well as abundance granting power through wholesome[1] nourishment.

49,11. But the deceitful of bad power, bad actions, bad words, bad religious views, and bad thought, (their) souls come to meet them with foul food. They will be real guests in the house of deceit.

49,12. What help do you have through truth, for Zarathushtra, who is calling (for you)? What do you have through good thought for me, who devote myself to you with praises, O Mazdā, entreating for that which is the best in your command?

End of Yasna 49

---

[1] 'wholesome': uncertain.

Yasna 50. Kat̰.mōi.uruuā Hāiti

50,1. Kat̰ mōi uruuā isē cahiiā auuaŋhō
kə̄ mōi pasə̄uš kə̄ mə̄.nā ϑrātā vistō
aniiō ašāt̰ ϑβat̰cā mazdā ahurā
azdā zūtā vahištāat̰cā manaŋhō

50,2. kaϑā mazdā rāniiō.skərəitīm° gąm išasōit̰
yə̄ hīm ahmāi vāstrauuaitīm stōi usiiāt̰
ərəžəjīš ašā pourušū huuarə̄ pišiiasū
ākāstə̄ŋg[1] mā nišąsiiā dāϑə̄m dāhuuā

50,3. at̰cīt̰ ahmāi mazdā ašā aŋhaitī
yąm hōi xšaϑrā vohucā cōišt manaŋhā
yə̄ nā ašōiš aojaŋhā varədaiiaētā
yąm nazdištąm gaēϑąm drəguuå baxšaitī

50,4. at̰ vå yazāi stauuas mazdå ahurā
hadā ašā vahištācā manaŋhā
xšaϑrācā yā īšō ståŋhat̰ ā paiϑī
ākå arədrə̄ṇg dəmānē garō sərao̧šānē

50,5. ārōi zī xšmā mazdå[2] ašā ahurā
hiiat̰ yūšmākāi mąϑrānē vaorāzaϑā
aibī.dərəštā āuuīšiiā auuaŋhā
zastāištā yā nå xᵛāϑrē dāiiāt̰

50,6. yə̄ mąϑrā vācəm mazdā baraitī
uruuaϑō ašā nəmaŋhā zaraϑuštrō
dātā xratə̄uš hizuuō raiϑīm stōi
mahiiā rāzə̄ṇg vohū sāhīt̰ manaŋhā

50,7. at̰ və̄ yaojā zəuuīštiiə̄ṇg auruuatō
jaiiāiš pərəϑūš vahmahiiā yūšmākahiiā
mazdā ašā ugrə̄ṇg vohū manaŋhā
yāiš azāϑā mahmāi x́iiātā auuaŋ́hē°

50,8. mat̰ vå padāiš yā frasrūtā īžaiiå
pairijasāi mazdā ustānazastō
at̰ vå ašā arədrax́iiācā nəmaŋhā
at̰ vå vaŋhə̄uš manaŋhō hunarətātā

[1] akāstə̄ṇg, i.e. akās-təṇg.
[2] mazdå, Geldner mazdā.

Yasna 50. Kat-mōi-urvā Hāiti

50,1. Does my soul[1] command any help? Who has been found as a protector of my cattle and myself, other than truth, you O Mazda Ahurā, and best thought, who quickly appear?

50,2. How, O Mazdā, should one try to win the joy-giving cow if he wishes her to be his, provided with pasture, one who lives decently with truth among the many who block the sun?[2] Facing these I shall settle down.[3] Do accept the just one.

50,3. Through truth, O Mazdā, the neighboring possession(s) shall belong to the man who could increase them by the strength of a reward, (the possessions) which have been assigned to him with power and good thought and which the deceitful one must (therefore) give up.

50,4. I will worship you, praising you, O Mazdā Ahura, along with truth and best thought and with the power by which one can tread upon the path of invigoration. Facing the zestful ones I wish to be heard in the house of song.

50,5. Since you delight in visible and manifest help for your manthra-keeper, (rewards) coming from your hands have been allotted by you, O Ahura (who are) Mazdā through truth, (rewards) which will put us in comfort.

50,6. The manthra-keeper who raises his voice in reverence, your ally in truth, O Mazdā, (is) Zarathushtra. May the Giver of Intellect instruct my tongue with good thought to be a charioteer of my prayer.[4]

50,7. With truth, I shall yoke for you the swiftest steeds of your glorification, O Mazdā, broad(chested) through victories and strong with good thought. With these (steeds) you shall drive hither. May you be present to help me.

50,8. I will approach you with footsteps celebrated as those of (personified) abundance,[5] with hands out-stretched with truth, O Mazdā, and with the reverence of a zestful person and with the skill of good thought.

[1] 'does my soul' is virtually the same as 'do I'.
[2] 'block the sun': uncertain.
[3] 'I shall settle down': uncertain.
[4] 'my tongue ... a charioteer of my prayer': Praying is compared with driving a chariot in a horse-race (Introd. 5.3).
[5] 'footsteps ... of (personified) abundance' alludes to a Proto-Aryan myth known from Vedic texts.

50,9. tāiš vå yasnāiš paitī stauuas aiienī
mazdā aṣ̌ā vaŋhə̄uš š́iiaoϑanāiš manaŋhō
yadā aṣ̌ōiš maẋiiå vasə̄ xšaiiā
at̰ hudānaoš[1] išaiiąs gərəzdā ẋiiə̄m

50,10. at̰ yā varəšā yācā pairī āiš š́iiaoϑanā
yācā vohū cašmąm arəjat̰ manaŋhā
raocå xᵛə̄ṇg asnąm uxšā aēuruš
xšmākāi aṣ̌ā vahmāi mazdā ahurā

50,11. at̰ və̄ staotā aojāi mazdā aŋhācā
yauuat̰ aṣ̌ā tauuācā isāicā
dātā aŋhə̄uš arədat̰ vohū manaŋhā
haiϑiiāuuarəštąm hiiat̰ vasnā fərašō.təməm

End of Yasna 50

[1] hudānaoš, Geldner hudānāuš.

50,9. With worships such as these, I will come to you again, O Mazdā, praising you, with truth and actions of good thought, when I have command at will of my reward. May I thus enjoy vigor in the grace of a generous person.

50,10. The actions which I shall perform and the actions performed by those all around here, as well as the things which deserve (to be seen by) eyes with good thought, the lights of the sun, the leading bull of the days,[1] all these are for your glorification with truth, O Mazdā Ahura.

50,11 I shall declare myself your praiser, O Mazdā, and I will remain so for as long as I can and am able through truth. Let the Giver of Existence promote through good thought the making real of what is most brilliant in value.

End of Yasna 50

[1] 'the leading bull of the days', i.e. the rosy dawn, cf. 46,3.

Yasna 51: Vohuxšaϑrā Gāϑā
=
Vohuxšaϑrā Hāiti

51,1. Vohū xšaϑrəm vairīm bāgəm aibī.bairištəm
vīdīšəmnāi[1] īžācit̰ aṣ̌ā aṇtarə caraitī
š́iiaoϑanāiš mazdā vahištəm tat̰ nə̄ nūcit̰ varəšānē

51,2. tā və̄ mazdā paouruuīm ahurā aṣ̌āi.yecā[2]
taibiiācā ārmaitē dōišā mōi ištōiš xšaϑrəm
xšmākəm vohū manaŋhā vahmāi dāidī sauuaŋhō

51,3. ā və̄ gəuš.ā° hə̄miiaṇtū yōi və̄ š́iiaoϑanāiš sārəṇtē
ahurō aṣ̌ā hizuuā[3] uxδāiš vaŋhə̄uš manaŋhō
yaēšąm tū pouruiiō mazdā fradaxštā ahī

51,4. kuϑrā ārōiš ā fsəratuš[4] kuϑrā mərəždikā axštat̰
kuϑrā yasō.x́iiən aṣ̌əm kū spəṇtā ārmaitiš
kuϑrā manō vahištəm kuϑrā ϑβā xšaϑrā mazdā

51,5. vīspā tā pərəsąs yaϑā aṣ̌āt̰ hacā gąm vīdat̰
vāstriiō š́iiaoϑanāiš ərəšuuō hąs huxratuš nəmaŋhā
yə̄ dāϑaēibiiō ərəš.ratūm xšaiiąs aṣ̌iuuā̊ cistā

51,6. yə̄ vahiiō vaŋhə̄uš dazdē yascā hōi vārāi rādat̰
ahurō xšaϑrā mazdā̊ at̰ ahmāi akāt̰ ašiiō
yə̄ hōi nōit̰ vīdāitī apə̄mē aŋhə̄uš uruuaēsē

51,7. dāidī mōi yə̄ gąm tašō apascā uruuarā̊scā
amərətātā hauruuātā spə̄ništā mainiiū mazdā
təuuīšī utaiiūitī manaŋhā vohū sə̄ŋ́hē°

51,8. at̰ zī tōi vaxšiiā mazdā vīdušē zī nā mruiiāt̰
hiiat̰ akōiiā drəguuāitē uštā yə̄ aṣ̌əm dādrē
huuō zī mąϑrā š́iiātō yə̄ vīdušē mrauuaitī

---

[1] vīdīšəmnāi, Geldner vīdīšəmnaiš.
[2] aṣ̌āi.yecā for aṣ̌āiiacā.
[3] hizuuā, Geldner hizuuā̊.
[4] ā fsəratuš, Geldner āfsəratuš.

Yasna 51. Vohukhshathrā Gātha

=

Vohukshathrā Hāiti

51,1. The good power worthy of being chosen, which brings most share(s) (and which is) best through actions, comes to the person liberal even with abundance, through truth. This (power), O Mazdā, I will procure for us now.

51,2. Therefore I will first show the power of my command to you, O Mazdā Ahura, and to truth, and to you, O right-mindedness. (Then) grant your (power) with good thought to the glorification of (your) benefaction.

51,3. O you, (who are) the Ahura through truth, let your ears reach those who associate with you by (their) actions[1] and by the utterances of good thought (spoken) by tongue, whose first teacher you are, O Mazdā.

51,4. Where will joy (arise) from a pious person? Where will it arise with compassion? Where do people honor truth? Where is holy right-mindedness? Where is best thought? Where, through your power, are they, O Mazdā?

51,5. I am asking about all this: how a herdsman obtains a cow in accordance with truth, being a nobleman through his actions and being of good intellect, in reverence (to Him) who, exercising power and holding rewards, finds a correct judgment for those who are just.

51,6. (To the person) who has accepted the very best[2] and who heeds His will, the Ahura with His power (will present Himself) as Mazdā.[3]. But what is the very worst[4] will (befall) the person who does not care for Him, at the final turning point of (his) existence.[5]

51,7. You, O Mazdā, who fashioned the cow, the waters, and the plants, grant me immortality and integrity through the most holy spirit, strength and stability through good thought at the pronouncement (of your judgment).

51,8. Now I shall tell you, O Mazdā, since a man would like to speak to the Knowing one, that in the evil for the deceitful one (lie things) desired by him who holds truth. That manthra-keeper is happy indeed who can speak to a knowing one.

---

[1] 'who associate with you by (their) actions', or: 'who are sheltered by your actions'?
[2] 'the very best', lit. 'what is better than good)'.
[3] '(will present Himself) as Mazda', i.e. '(will present Himself) as wise'.
[4] 'the very worst', lit. 'what is worse than evil'.
[5] 'at the final turning point of (his) existence' (individual judgment), or: 'at the final turning point of existence/world' (universal judgment)?

51,9. yąm xšnūtəm rānōibiiā dā̊   ϑβā āϑrā suxrā mazdā
aiiaŋhā xšustā aibī   ahuuāhū daxštəm dāuuōi
rāšaiieŋ́hē drəguuaṇtəm   sauuaiiō aṣ̌auuanəm

51,10. at̰ yə̄ mā nā marəxšaitē   aniiāϑā ahmāt̰ mazdā
huuō dāmōiš drūjō hunuš   tā duždā̊ yōi hə̄ṇtī
maibiiō zbaiiā aṣ̌əm   vaŋhuiiā aṣ̌ī gat̰.tē[1]

51,11. kə̄ uruuaϑō spitamāi   zaraϑuštrāi nā mazdā
kə̄ vā aṣ̌ā āfraštā   kā spəṇtā ārmaitiš
kə̄ vā vaŋhə̄uš manaŋhō   acistā magāi ərəšuuō

51,12. nōit̰ tā īm xšnāuš vaēipiiō°   kəuuīnō pərətā̊[2] zimō[3]
zaraϑuštrəm spitāməm   hiiat̰ ahmī urūraost aštō
hiiat̰ hōi īm caratascā   aodərəšcā zōišənū vāzā

51,13. tā drəguuatō marədaitī[4]   daēnā ərəzaoš[5] haiϑīm
yehiiā uruuā xraodaitī   cinuuatō pərətā̊ ākā̊
xᵛāiš šiiaoϑanāiš hizuuascā   aṣ̌ahiiā nąsuuā̊ paϑō

51,14. nōit̰ uruuāϑā dātōibiiascā   karapanō vāstrāt̰ arə̄m
gauuōi ārōiš āsə̄ṇdā   xᵛāiš šiiaoϑanāiš sə̄ṇghāišcā
yə̄ īš sə̄ṇghō apə̄məm   drūjō dəmānē ādāt̰

51,15. hiiat̰ mīždəm zaraϑuštrō   magauuabiiō cōišt parā
garō dəmānē ahurō   mazdā̊ jasat̰ pouruiiō
tā və̄ vohū manaŋhā   aṣ̌āicā sauuāiš cəuuišī[6]

51,16. tąm kauuā vīštāspō   magahiiā xšaϑrā nąsat̰
vaŋhə̄uš padəbīš manaŋhō   yąm cistīm aṣ̌ā maṇtā
spəṇtō mazdā̊ ahurō   aϑā nə̄ sazdiiāi uštā

51,17. bərəxδąm mōi fərašaoštrō   huuō.guuō daēdōišt kəhrpə̄m
daēnaiiāi vaŋhuiiāi   yąm hōi išiiąm dātū
xšaiiąs mazdā ahurā   aṣ̌ahiiā āždiiāi gərəzdīm

51,18. tąm cistīm də̄jāmāspō   huuō.guuō ištōiš xᵛarənā̊
aṣ̌ā vərəṇtē tat̰ xšaϑrəm   manaŋhō vaŋhə̄uš[7] vīdō
tat̰ mōi dāidī ahurā   hiiat̰ mazdā rapə̄n tauuā

---

[1] gat̰.te, i.e. gate.
[2] pərətā̊, slightly incorrect for pərətāu, Geldner pərətō.
[3] zimō, Geldner zəmō.
[4] marədaitī with Geldner, or: marədaite?
[5] ərəzaoš, Geldner ərəzāuš.
[6] cəuuišī, Geldner ciuuīšī.
[7] vaŋhə̄uš, Geldner vaŋuhīš (i.e. vaŋᵛhīš).

51,9. Make clear (to them) in (their) minds, O Mazdā, which (is) the gratification you apportion with your red fire and the molten metal according to the balance. In order to damage the deceitful one you benefit the truthful one.

51,10. The man who unlike the (trutfhul one) tries to destroy me, O Mazdā, that man is the brat of the originator of deceit. Therefore he gives bad gifts (to those) who exist. I invoke truth to come to me with a good reward.

51,11. Who is the man (who can be) an ally of Spitama Zarathushtra, O Mazdā? Who took counsel with truth? With whom did holy right-mindedness (take counsel)? Which nobleman recognized (Zarathushtra) for the offering of good thought?

51,12. Residing at (his) bridge, Vaēpiya the Kaviyan did not gratify Spitama Zarathushtra when as a messenger he stopped there in winter and (was offered there) two horrible 'gifts of hospitality', (showing him) the door-step and (leaving him in shivery) cold.

51,13. In such a way the religious view of a deceitful person will miss the reality of the straight (path). His soul, facing (him) at the Account-keeper's Bridge, will make him tremble, for he has strayed from the path of truth by his own actions and those of his tongue.

51,14. The Karapans are not allied with the laws and (the orders of) the pasture. By their own actions and proclamations they are hostile to the cow of the pious person. In the end, such proclamation will put them in the house of deceit.

51,15. In the house of song, Ahura Mazdā, the Primal one, comes to the faithful offerers (with) the prize that Zarathushtra promised them. Therefore I commit myself to you, and to truth, with good thought on account of (your) benefactions.[1]

51,16. Kavi Vishtāspa, by his power over the offering, (proceeding) on the paths of good thought, has reached that insight which holy Mazdā Ahura has conceived with truth. Thus he may proclaim to us the things desired.

51,17. Frashaoshtra Hvōguva dedicates his esteemed self[2] to my Good Religion.[3] Let Mazdā Ahura, who exercises the power, make it[4] vigorous for him, so that he may reach the grace of truth.

51,18 With truth, Jāmāspa Hvōguva, in his quest for glories, chooses that insight and that power (which is that) of the possession of good thought. Grant me, O Mazdā, O Supporter, that (power) which is yours.

---

[1] The end of the stanza is uncertain.
[2] 'his esteemed self', lit. 'his esteemed body'.
[3] 'my Good Religion', cf. 53,1 'his Good Religion', and 53,4 'the Good Religion'.
[4] 'it', i.e. his esteemd self/body, or: the Good Religion?

51,19. huuō tat̰ nā maidiiōi.mąŋhā spitamā ahmāi dazdē
daēnaiiā vaēdəmnō yə̄ ahūm išasąs aibī
mazdā̊ dātā mraot̰ gaiiehiiā šiiaoϑanāiš vahiiō

51,20. tat̰ vō nə̄ hazaošā̊ŋhō vīspā̊ŋhō daidiiāi sauuō
aṣ̌əm vohū manaŋhā uxδā yāiš ārmaitiš
yazəmnā̊ŋhō nəmaŋhā mazdā̊ rafəδrəm cagədō

51,21. ārmatōiš nā spəṇtō huuō cistī uxδāiš šiiaoϑanā
daēnā aṣ̌əm spə̄nuuat̰ vohū xšaϑrəm manaŋhā
mazdā̊ dadāt̰ ahurō tə̄m vaŋᵛhīm° yāsā aṣ̌īm

51,22. yehiiā mōi aṣ̌āt̰ hacā vahištəm yesnē paitī
vaēdā mazdā̊ ahurō yōi ā̊ŋharəcā həṇticā
tą yazāi xᵛāiš nāmə̄nīš pairicā jasāi vaṇtā

End of Yasna 51

51,19 O Maidyōimāngha Spitama, that man who, in his desire for winning existence, recites the laws of Mazdā obtains that (power) which he (already) possesses in his religious view and which, through the actions of the living, is the better one.

51,20. In order for all of you to grant us in harmony that benefit we worship truth with good thought as well as the utterances with which right-mindedness (is associated), (worshipping them) in reverence for Mazdā who extends support.

51,21. By virtue of right-mindedness, this holy man[1] makes truth prosper through the utterances (inspired) by his insight, through his action and his religious view. Mazdā Ahura grants power through good thought. I entreat Him for a good reward.

51,22. Mazdā Ahura knows (the person) whose best (attitude is seen) by me at worship, in accordance with truth. Those who have existed and exist, (those) I will worship with my own (people) by (calling their) names, and I shall approach them with affection.[2]

End of Yasna 51

[1] 'this holy man', i.e. 'Zarathushtra'.
[2] Cf. 27,15 (Yenghē Hātām).

Yasna 53: Vahištōišti Gāϑā

=

Vahištōišti Hāiti

53,1. Vahištā īštiš srāuuī zaraϑuštrahē
spitāmahiiā yezī hōi dāt̰ āiiaptā
aṣ̌āt̰ hacā ahurō mazdā̊ yauuōi vīspāi.ā huuaŋhəuuīm
yaēcā hōi dabən[1] saš̌ənçā[2] daēnaiiā̊ vaŋhuiiā̊ uxδā š́iiaoϑanācā

53,2. at̰cā hōi scantū manaŋhā uxδāiš š́iiaoϑanāišcā
xšnəm[3] mazdā̊ vahmāi.ā fraorət̰ yasnąscā
kauuacā vīštāspō zaraϑuštriš spitāmō fərašaoštrascā
dā̊ŋhō ərəzūš paϑō yąm daēnąm ahuro saošiiantō dadāt̰

53,3. təmcā tū pourucistā haēcat̰.aspānā
spitāmī yezuuī[4] dugədrąm zaraϑuštrahē
vaŋhəuš paitiiāstī[m][5] manaŋhō aṣ̌ahiiā mazdā̊scā taibiiō dāt̰ sarəm
aϑā həm.fərašuuā ϑβā xraϑβā spəništā ārmatōiš hudānū° varəšuua[6]

53,4. təm zī və spərədā niuuarānī[7] yā fəδrōi vīdāt̰
paiϑiiaēcā vāstriiaēibiiō at̰cā x'aētauuē°
aṣ̌āunī aṣ̌auuabiiō manaŋhō vaŋhəuš x'ənuuat̰ haŋhuš məm.bəəduš[8]
mazdā̊ dadāt̰ ahurō daēnaiiāi vaŋhuiiāi yauuōi vīspāi.ā

53,5. sāx'ənī vaziiamnābiiō kainibiiō mraomī
xšmaibiiācā vadəmnō mənçā ī [mąz]dazdūm
vaēdō.dūm° daēnābīš abiiascā[9] ahūm yə̄ vaŋhəuš manaŋhō
aṣ̌ā və aniiō ainīm vīuuə̄ŋhatū tat̰ zī hōi hušənəm aŋhat̰

53,6. iϑā ī haiϑiiā narō aϑā jənaiiō
drūjō hacā rāϑəmō yə̄mə spašuϑā frāidīm
[drūjō] āiiesē hōi-‹ī›š[10] piϑā tanuuō parā
vaiiū bərədbiiō[11] duš.x'arəϑəm nąsat̰ x'āϑrəm
drəguuō.dəbiiō° dəjīt̰.arətaēibiiō anāiš ā manahīm ahūm mərəngəduiiē

---

[1] dabən, perhaps incorrect for dadən, but var. dəbən, dbən, dabin.
[2] saš̌ənçā for slightly incorrect saškənçā of the mss. and Geldner.
[3] xšnəm, Geldner xšnūm.
[4] yezuuī, Geldner yeziuuī.
[5] paitiiāstīm manaŋhō for paitiiastī manaŋhō owing to erroneous segmentation of the spoken text; Geldner paitiiāstəm.
[6] hudānū varəšuuā, Geldner hudānuuarəšuuā.
[7] spərədā niuuarānī, Geldner spərədānī varānī.
[8] məm.bəəduš blunder for mən.bənduš?
[9] abiiascā, Geldner abiiastā.
[10] hōi-‹ī›š for slightly incorrect hōiš of the mss..
[11] bərədbiiō, Geldner bərədubiiō.

Yasna 53. Vahishtōishti Gāthā

=

Vahishtōishti Hāiti

53,1. The best quest of Zarathushtra has found a hearing, since Mazdā Ahura, in accordance with truth, has granted the boons (of) good existence for all times, to him as well as to those who practice and master the utterances and actions of his Good Religion.

53,2. Let therefore Kavi Vishtāspa (as well as) Spitama the son of Zarathushtra, and Frashaoshtra join devotedly in the recognition of Mazdā for His glorification and in His worship with utterances and actions (inspired) by Zarathushtra's thought, thus pursuing the straight paths of offering, (following) the religious view that the Ahura has established to be that of a benefactor.

53,3. Pouruchistā Haēchataspānā Spitāmī, you young(est) among Zarathushtra's daughters, (your father) gives you such (benefactor) as shelter,[1] in obedience to good thought, truth, and Mazdā. Thus take counsel with your intellect. Choose[2] with (your) generous (groom) the holiest (things) of right-mindedness.

53,4. I want him to be cared for by you with that eagerness with which (a woman) shall care for her father and her husband, for the herdsmen and her family, as a truthful woman (cares) for truthful persons. Mazdā Ahura, valuing the bonds of kinship,[3] grants a sunny harvest of good thought to the Good Religion[4] for all times.

53,5. By speaking to you I give instructions to the nubile maidens and to all of you. (If) you note these (instructions) in your minds, (then) you will possess with your religious views and for their benefit the existence of good thought. May each of you try to surpass the other in truth, as this will be fruitful for him (and her).

53,6. In this respect, the (instructions) are true (for you), O men, and in that respect (for you), O women. As for the person who is dependent on deceit and whom you see having dishonest intentions,[5] I shall take away his defenses from his body. With the wind, comfort goes away from the deceitful oppressors of truth, who offer foul food. With these you destroy your spiritual existence.[6]

---

[1] The Middle Persian tradition suggests that the Vahishtōishti Gātha was composed by the prophet on the occasion of the marriage of his youngest daughter Poruchistā with Jāmāspa. Yet, strangely enough, the name of Jāmāspa is not mentioned in the Gātha. To justify tradition we assume that the name of the bridegroom is passed over in silence for apotropaeic or similar reasons.
[2] 'choose', or: 'make for yourself'?
[3] 'valuing the bonds of kinship': uncertain.
[4] 'to the Good Religion', i.e. 'to (the adherents of) the Good Religion'.
[5] 'having dishonest intentions': uncertain.
[6] 'spiritual existence', lit. 'mental existence', i.e. 'existence of thought'.

53,7. at̰cā və̄ mīždəm aŋhat̰ ahiiā magahiiā
yauuat̰ āžuš zrazdištō° būnōi haxtiiā̊°
paracā mraocąs aorācā yaϑrā mainiiuš drəguuatō anąsat̰ parā
vīzaiiaϑā[1] magə̄m tə̄m at̰ və̄ vaiiōi aŋhaitī apə̄məm vacō

53,8. anāiš ā dužuuarəšnaŋhō dafšniiā hə̄n̦tū
zaxiiācā vīspā̊ŋhō xraosən̦tąm upā
huxšaϑrāiš jə̄nərąm xrūnərąmcā rāmąmcā āiš dadātū šiieitibiiō vīžibiiō
īratū īš duuafšo huuō dərəzā mərəiϑiiaoš[2] mazištō mošucā astū

53,9. dužuuarənāiš vaēšō rāstī tōi narəpīš rajīš[3]
aēšasā də̄jīt̰.arətā pəšō.tanuuō
kū aṣ̌auuā ahurō yə̄ īš jiiātə̄uš hə̄miϑiiāt̰ vasə̄.itōišcā
tat̰ mazdā tauuā xšaϑrəm yā ərəžəjiiōi dāhī drigauuē° vahiiō

End of Yasna 53

[1] vīzaiiaϑā, Geldner ivīzaiiaϑā.
[2] mərəiϑiiaoš, Geldner mərəϑiiāuš.
[3] rajīš, Geldner arəjīš.

53,7. For this offering there will be a prize for you. The very faithful one will keep off[1] disease from the depth of his body[2] whereas the deceitful one, going back and down, will lose his spirit(s). If you do not partake in this offering then 'woe' will be your last word.

53,8. Let the evil-doers be knocked down by those (who are truthful), and let them (all) get exhausted howling upwards. Through good rulers wielding power over the killers and blood-shedders let one establish peace with the (evil-doers) for the settled villages. Let the greatest harm come upon them with the fetter(s) of death, and let it come soon.

53,9. Rot spreads through those of evil preferences. They are (nothing but) dusk and darkness, greedy violators of truth whose bodies are forfeited. Where is the truthful Ahura who may deprive them of their livelihood and liberty? It is your power, O Mazdā, through which you will grant what is better to the poor person living decently.

End of Yasna 53

[1] 'will keep off', or: 'will yoke', or: 'as long as'?
[2] This translation is most doubtful.

Yasna 54,1. Conclusion

Ā Airiiəmā Išiiō

Ā airiiəmā išiiō rafəδrāi jaṇtū
nərəbiiascā nāiribiiascā zaraϑuštrahē
vaŋhəuš rafəδrāi manaŋhō
yā daēnā vairīm hanāṯ mīždəm
aṣ̌ahiiā yāsā aṣ̌īm
yąm išiiąm ahurō masatā mazdå

End

Yasna 54,1. Conclusion

Ā Airyēmā Ishiyō

Let the vigorous people (of Vishtāspa)[1]
come to the support of the men and women of Zarathushtra,
to the support of good thought,
(following) the religious view that will deserve a prize worthy of being chosen.
I ask for the invigorating reward of truth, which Mazda Ahura has devised.

End

[1] 'the vigorous people' (lit. 'the vigorous tribe'), or: 'the invigorating people', i.e. 'the people provided with invigoration' (cf. 32,16). Note the repetition 'vigorous ... invigorating'.